MEDIAEVAL RELIGION
AND OTHER ESSAYS

MEDIAEVAL RELIGION
(THE FORWOOD LECTURES 1934)
AND OTHER ESSAYS

* *
*

BY

CHRISTOPHER DAWSON

NEW YORK
SHEED & WARD INC.
1934

FIRST PUBLISHED OCTOBER 1934
BY SHEED AND WARD, INC.
FROM 63 FIFTH AVENUE
NEW YORK CITY

2ND IMPRESSION NOVEMBER 1934
PRINTED IN THE U. S. A.
BY THE POLYGRAPHIC COMPANY OF AMERICA
NEW YORK CITY

PREFATORY NOTE

THE four lectures on Religion and Mediaeval Culture which make up the main part of this book consist of the Forwood Lectures which I delivered at Liverpool University during the early part of the present year. I have added two other essays bearing on the same subject. The first of these, which gives fuller treatment to one of the main theses of my fourth lecture, appeared as an article in the *Criterion* for January 1932. The other, an essay on William Langland, appeared in a volume of essays on English types of sanctity, entitled *The English Way*.

I wish to thank the Editor of the *Criterion* for permission to include the article on *The Origins of the Romantic Tradition*.

C.D.

CONTENTS

★ ★
★

vii

RELIGION AND MEDIAEVAL CULTURE

I
THE SOCIOLOGICAL FOUNDATIONS

1

THE study of mediaeval religion is of primary importance alike for those who wish to know something of the history of Christianity and for those who wish to know something of the history of Europe. We cannot understand the religious problems of the world to-day unless we understand something of their roots in the history of the past, and we cannot understand the secular history of modern Europe, unless we understand something of that long thousand-year process of change and growth which we name the Middle Ages. Those thousand years saw the making of Europe and the birth and rebirth of Western culture; they also witnessed the creation of that socio-religious unity that we call Christendom, and the gradual penetration of our culture by Christian beliefs and Christian moral and intellectual standards. They have left an indelible imprint on both our social and religious life. They have helped to make us what we are, whether for good or for evil, and even those who know and care nothing about mediaeval religion and culture, are themselves the unconscious heirs of mediaeval traditions.

It is true that the continuity of the European tradition was apparently broken by the conscious reaction against mediaeval culture and religion which occurred in the age of the Renaissance and the Reformation. The Humanists regarded the Middle Ages as a 'dark age' of Gothic barbarism, while to the Reformers they seemed an age of spiritual darkness and superstition which hardly deserved to be called Christian at all. Both parties agreed in wishing to cut out the last thousand years of history and to start again from classical culture on the one hand, and from primitive Christianity on the other.

Nevertheless this break with the past was far less complete than the makers of it believed. The Reformers and their successors the Puritans were not early Christians but post-mediaeval men who had a great deal in common with their immediate ancestors, while in the case of the Renaissance it is becoming increasingly clear that the new thought of the new age, whether it be the philosophy of Descartes, the science of Copernicus, the drama of Shakespeare, or the poetry of Spenser, has far closer links with the mediaeval past than their makers themselves realized. Thus the sixteenth-century reaction against the Middle Ages did not really destroy the continuity of our culture, or wipe out our debt to the Middle Ages; what it did do, however, was to place an artificial barrier between the European mind and mediaeval culture and religion, and to make the appreciation of the latter impossible for centuries. This was not peculiar to Protestant Europe, it was almost equally characteristic of Catholic countries in the post Renaissance period, and it was not until the coming of the Romantic movement in the nineteenth century, and of the new school of history that had its origin in Romanticism, that a genuine appreciation of mediaeval culture became possible. In fact the Protestant prejudice against mediaeval religion seems to have been a less serious factor than the intellectual and aesthetic prejudices of Humanism. In other words the real cause of modern misunderstanding and lack of appreciation of the mediaeval tradition has been cultural rather than religious. No doubt it is always difficult to understand the religion of the past without some knowledge of contemporary culture, but this is above all the case in periods like the Middle Ages, when religion and civilization were so closely united that religious institutions were the main organs of culture and almost every form of social activity possessed a religious sanction. In order to understand the religion of such an age, it is not enough to study it theologically in its essential dogmas and religious principles, it is also necessary to study it sociologically with reference to the changing complex of social traditions and cultural institutions into which it became incorporated. The social form of a religion depends not only on the inner logic of its moral doctrine, but on the type of culture with which it is united, and also on the way in which its union with the culture is achieved. In the first place a religion may grow up, as it were naturally, with the life of a people, so as to seem inseparable from it. This is the normal process in the case of primitive cultures and it is often the case with more advanced types of civilization, as with the Greeks and the Romans.

In the second place a religion may enter a fully formed culture from without, as Buddhism entered China or as Islam conquered Persia in the seventh century. Finally we have the case of a religion already fully formed entering a culture which is still in process of formation and thus itself becoming one of the constituent elements of the new culture that is growing up.

The history of mediaeval Christianity is the classic example of this third process, and it is exceptionally worthy of study not only on account of its influence on the development of the modern world, but also owing to the peculiar complexity of the process itself and the number of factors that are involved. For Christianity did not come to the peoples of northern and western Europe out of the void, as Islam came to Western Asia in the seventh century, it already had a long history behind it. To the northern barbarians Christianity was the religion of the Roman Empire and to them it stood for the Latin order with all its heritage of law and civilization. To the Romans themselves, however, even in the fifth century Christianity was comparatively a new comer. It came to them from the Hellenistic East, its mother tongue was Greek and its theological development was mainly the work of the Greek Fathers and the Greek councils. And finally the Greek-speaking world itself possessed a double tradition. The schools of Athens still maintained what they believed to be the pure Hellenic tradition of culture and looked on Christianity as a modern intruder, while the Christians themselves claimed to be the spiritual heirs not of Greece but of Israel, and of an historic religious tradition which had its roots deep in the past of the ancient East.

All these currents of religious and social tradition met in the main stream of Catholic Christianity which now flowed out into the barbarous West. Was this great river of sacred tradition to become lost in the swamps and forests of the North? or was it destined to irrigate the virgin soil and make it capable of bearing as rich a spiritual harvest as the highly cultivated lands of the Eastern Mediterranean? That was the great problem which the early mediaeval Church had to face, and its essential preoccupation was how to preserve its

spiritual inheritance so that nothing was lost and so
that the same faith and the same life should be followed
by the northern barbarians as by the educated classes of
the later Roman Empire.

Many different views have been held as to the measure
of success which the Church attained in carrying out this
task, but there can be no question of the vast moral effort
that it entailed or that this effort was one of the great formative spiritual powers in the making of Western culture. At first sight it might seem that the task was almost
a hopeless one, for the German warrior and the Celtic
peasant looked on the world with other eyes than did
the civilized Roman magistrate or the Greek scholar or
the oriental ascetic, and there was nothing in their culture and their social traditions that could help them to
understand the religious thought and the moral ideals
of the civilized Christian world of the patristic age.
Thanks however to the existence of the Church and
the ecclesiastical order, Christianity was not abandoned passively to the influences of its social environment.
It had its own principle of order, its own social organs
and its own civic traditions. Christianity was not merely a doctrine and a life, it was, above all, a society, and it
was the organic unity and continuity of the Christian
society which preserved the spiritual identity of the
Christian religion. Had it not been for the existence of
this firm juridical and institutional organization, there
can be little doubt that Christianity would have changed its nature in changing its social environment and
would have become to all intents and purposes a different religion.

We can trace the beginnings of such a development

in the Arianism of the Goths and the Vandals, which
was due to political rather than theological causes and
which seemed likely to become the national religion of
the Germanic peoples. Even in the short period of their
existence these churches seem to have acquired a distinctive national type of organization. Their clergy
were attached to the chief and to the army rather than
to diocesan sees, and St Ambrose describes the Gothic
bishop, with his barbaric necklaces and arm bands going before the army like the priests of the old heathen
cult whose place he had taken.[1] Modern German
writers such as Stutz and von Schubert[2] regard this
'nationalization' of Christianity as typical not only of
the Gothic Arians but of the Germanic peoples in general, and as supplying a key to the changes in ecclesiastical organization and institutions which marked the
new age. No doubt other influences were at work. For
example the development of lay ownership of churches and abbeys, which these writers regard as a typically
German institution, like the private sanctuary of Nordic paganism, seems rather to be due to the tendency of
landlords in the Roman Empire no less than in the barbarian kingdoms to treat the churches on their do-
mains as private property.[3]

Nevertheless the differences in sociological structure
that distinguished the barbarian kingdoms from the old

---

[1] *Ep.* 10, cap. 9.

[2] V. Stutz, *Geschichte des Kirchlichen Benefizialwesens,* I, 1895,
and his articles *Eigenkirche, Eigenkloster* in Hauck's *Realenzyklo-
paedie,* 1913.

[3] Cf. Lesne, *Histoire de la propriété ecclésiastique en France,* I, 70-
78 (1910).

imperial society could not fail to have an effect upon the Church itself. The Church of the Empire had been a church of the cities. Its organization was based upon the municipal system, and the bishop played an even more important part in the life of the city than the civil magistrates themselves. The larger the city, the greater, as a rule, was its ecclesiastical importance, as for example in Egypt where Alexandria was the one great ecclesiastical centre and its bishop exercised almost absolute control over the whole country.

Among the Germanic and Celtic peoples, however, social conditions were entirely different. City life was non-existent and the only units were the people, or the tribes and their subdivisions.

Here the Church could find no fixed centres on which to concentrate its action and from which to radiate its influence. It was forced either to create such centres for itself through the foundation of monasteries which in the Celtic countries became the basis of the whole ecclesiastical organization, or else to make the tribal territory or petty kingdom itself an episcopal see, as we find in many cases in Anglo-Saxon England.

In the Frankish kingdom, where the city and the city territories survived, the Church was able to preserve its old basis of organization, but even here the decay of urban life and the disappearance of the old provincial organization destroyed the cohesion and autonomy of the hierarchy and brought them into dependence on the royal power. The Church became more and more closely bound up with the life of the state. It ceased to be simply a province of the international Christian society and became a territorial church (or what the

Germans call a *landeskirche*). This development was not however entirely due to the growing dependence of the Church upon the state, it also involved a corresponding dependence of the state upon the Church. The trained bureaucracy which had been the strength of the later Roman Empire no longer existed, and the clergy was the only remaining class which could provide the state with educated councillors and administrators.

In all the western kingdoms the bishops took a leading part in the royal councils and national assemblies, while in England and Spain the Kings and secular magnates also took part in the ecclesiastical councils: indeed in Visigothic Spain the great councils of Toledo were true national assemblies which exercised legislative and judicial functions even in secular affairs. In Gaul the Merovingian kings, for all their violence and tyranny, recognized what they owed to the support and co-operation of the Church and paid their debt by lavish grants of territory and all kinds of fiscal and judicial privileges. It has been calculated that by the close of the seventh century the Church owned no less than a third of the soil of France, and whatever may be the exact proportion there can be no doubt about the enormous agrarian wealth of the Church or of the change in social and economic conditions that this involved. The Church had ceased to be urban and had become agrarian. All over western Europe it had sunk its roots deep in the soil. The bishops had become great territorial magnates who governed their estates like princes and levied not only tithes and ecclesiastical dues but also tolls and taxes.

Obviously the royal power could not afford to neglect so vast a source of wealth and power. From the beginning the Frankish rulers attempted to control episcopal elections for their own ends until in the eighth century bishoprics and abbacies were used by Charles Martel in order to provide his relatives and partisans with rich benefices even though they were laymen. This marks perhaps the lowest point to which the Frankish Church descended. It had become so closely identified with the territorial state that it had lost its spiritual autonomy and seemed bound to be swamped by the flood of barbarism in which it was sinking.

It was clear that the territorial church did not possess sufficient inherent vitality to react against its barbaric environment and to create a genuinely Christian culture. For this it was necessary that there should be a reassertion of the universalist principles that were of the very essence of Western Catholicism—a revival alike of the ecclesiastical order and of the ecclesiastical culture, both of which had been impaired by the centrifugal development of the national or territorial churches of the West. The reassertion of these principles was due to the intervention of the Papacy, which had retained its position as the organ of unity and the guardian of Catholic tradition in spite of the fall of the Empire. Rome still remained nominally a part of the Empire and thus held an intermediate position between East and West, between the Byzantine and the Germanic worlds. But while the Papacy enjoyed immense prestige in the West both as the heir of the traditions of imperial Rome and as the Apostolic See of St Peter, it had no power to make its authority effective and consequently was little more than the shadow of a great name in the ecclesiastical affairs of the new kingdoms. It is true that the Bishop of Arles held the title of Vicar of the Holy See, and thus supplied a link and a channel of communication between Rome and the Frankish Church. But Arles was itself little more than a relic of the Roman past, and had no real importance for the territorial Frankish Church. Between that Church and Rome stood not the Apostolic Vicar but the Frankish monarchy. No reform was possible without the consent of the latter, and since the royal interests were bound up with the existing abuses the problem of reform was not an easy one.

There was, however, a third element in the Western Church which provided the Papacy with the assistance of which it stood in need. Without the help of the monks the Papacy could never have made its authority effective in the West, while without the Papacy, the monks could have had little influence in the ecclesiastical organization of the territorial Churches. It was the union of these two powers which determined the evolution of the mediaeval church and restored its universal character. Purely oriental in its origins, the monastic life had been adapted to the needs of Western society and to the spirit of the Latin tradition by the work of St Benedict, and it was the biographer of St Benedict, the great monastic pope, St Gregory, who first enlisted the monks in the service of the universal church by entrusting to them the mission to the Anglo-Saxons which was the starting point of a new era in the history of the Western Church. Already in the North the Irish monks had begun to combine the monastic

life with an active missionary propaganda, both in
Britain and Gaul, and Anglo-Saxon monasticism inherited their traditions as well as those of St Benedict
and St Gregory. But it was the Roman and Benedictine
power which gave the new movement its organizing
power and its spirit of Christian universalism. The
Celtic monks on the continent had striven to emanci-
pate their monasteries from the control of the local
bishops and to make them independent of the territorial church organization, but the Anglo-Saxons brought
this autonomous tradition into direct relation with the
centre of Catholic unity. They were a disciplined army
under the orders of the Holy See for the service of the
universal church.

The climax of this development is to be seen in the
work of St Boniface, which marks an epoch in the history both of the territorial churches of Northern Europe and in that of the Papacy. For at the very moment
when these new prospects were opening to the Papacy
in the West, its traditional connection with the East
was being threatened by the iconoclastic policy of the
Isaurian emperors. Gregory II, the greatest of the Popes
between Gregory I and Nicholas I, showed a remarkable insight into the significance of what was taking
place. In his letters to the Emperor Leo, the genuine-
ness of which has recently been vindicated by Professor
Caspar, he appeals from the verdict of the Emperor
and the civilized Byzantine world to the new Christian
world that was coming into existence in the West, and
in order to show his independence of the former he announced his intention of leaving Rome on a journey
"to the innermost lands of the West" in order to bap-

tize the princes of the newly converted nations that
were bringing the first fruits of their faith to the see of
Peter.[4]

This journey never actually took place, but even if
the Pope had visited Germany in person he could not
have associated himself more decisively with the work
of St Boniface than he had already done in 722 when he
consecrated Boniface as bishop for Germany at large
in immediate dependence on the Holy See, and gave
him a mandate for the conversion of Germany. This
mandate was still further extended by Gregory II's
successors who made Boniface their legate and personal
representative and charged him not only with the
organization of the German Church but also with the
reform and reorganization of the territorial church of
the Frankish kingdom as a whole. Thus St Boniface
had a double mission to fulfil, and the way in which he

[4]"The whole West," he writes, "has its eyes fixed on our poor
person, and though we are unworthy of it yet they have great
confidence in us and in him whose image you would destroy
and abolish, the Holy Apostle Peter whom all the kingdoms of
the West reverence as a god upon earth." "You know your empire cannot insure control of Rome, apart from the city itself, on
account of the nearness of the sea and the ships, but the Pope has
only to depart three miles from Rome and he has no more to
fear from you. It grieves us that the savages and barbarians are
becoming tame while you, the civilized, are becoming barbarous. The whole of the West brings the fruits of its faith to the
Prince of the Apostles, and if you send troops for the destruction
of the images of St Peter, look to it. We warn you beforehand
that we are innocent of the blood that you will shed. Be it on
your own head." Cf. Caspar, *Geschichte des Papstums*, II, 656-
662, and more fully in *Zeitschrift für Kirchengeschichte*, vol. 52,
pp. 29 seq. (1933).

carried out his immense task almost gives him the right
to be called the founder of mediaeval Christendom.
In Germany he was the creator of a new Christian
order, not only by the formation of the new German
sees, but still more by the introduction of Anglo-
Saxon monks and nuns and their establishment as
colonists of Christian culture in the newly converted
territories of Central Germany. In Gaul he was the
apostle of Catholic universalism and canonical order,
and the reformer of the secularized and territorialized
church of the Frankish kingdom.

But while his apostolate in Germany was amazingly
fruitful, his efforts for the reform and reorganization
of the Frankish church were only partially successful.
The keystone of his programme of reform was the
restoration of the old metropolitan organization and
the centralization of the Church by the direct subordin-
ation of the metropolitans to Rome. As he wrote to the
Archbishop of Canterbury after the great Pan-Frank-
ish reform council of 747, "We decreed and acknowledged in our synod that we would preserve to the end
of our lives Catholic faith and unity and subjection to
the Roman Church: that we would be subject to St
Peter and his vicar; that we should convoke a synod
every year; that the metropolitans should seek their
palls from the Holy See, and that in all things we desired to follow the precepts of St Peter, according to
the canons, so as to be numbered among the sheep en-
trusted to him . . . We decreed that it was the business
of a metropolitan in accordance with canon law to ex-
amine the conduct of the bishops subordinate to him
and their care for their people; and that he should

warn the bishops on coming from the synods to meet
the priests and abbots in his own diocese and to enjoin
them to keep the decrees of the synod. And each bishop,
if there is anything in his diocese that he has been unable to correct or amend, should bring it before the
archbishop in the presence of all at the synod, in the
same way as the Roman Church bound us with an
oath to do when we were ordained, that if I saw priests
or people wandering from the way of God and was
unable to correct them, I should always faithfully
point it out for correction to the Apostolic See and the
vicar of St Peter. For so, if I am not mistaken, all the
Bishops should make known to the metropolitan whatever they are unable to correct in their people, and he
in like manner to the Roman pontiff, and so they will
be clear of the blood of lost souls."[5]

The realization of such a programme would have
cut across the existing organization of the territorial
church and would have deprived the state of the *de
facto* control over the church which it actually enjoyed.
The interests of the Frankish state were opposed to the
direct subjection of the metropolitans, and through
them of the national church, to the authority of Rome,
yet, as Boniface himself recognized, it was only by the
favour and help of the temporal power that the work
of reform and evangelization could be carried on. "For
without the protection of the prince of the Franks," he
writes to Bishop Daniel of Winchester, "I can neither
rule the people nor defend the priests or the deacons,
the monks or the handmaidens of God, nor without
his mandate and fear can I forbid the rites of the pagans

[5]S. Boniface, *Ep.* 78.

in Germany and their sacrilegious idolatry."[6] And thus the final result of Boniface's work was a compromise, which secured the reform of the Frankish Church, and its closer union with Rome, but which did so not by the canonical machinery of metropolitans and provincial synods and the appelate jurisdiction of the Holy See, but by the direct co-operation of the temporal power and through its controlling influence on the territorial church.

In fact Boniface was the unwilling agent of that alliance between the Papacy and the Frankish monarchy which did so much to determine the course of mediaeval history, but which was fatal to Boniface's own ideal of ecclesiastical independence It led to the separation of the Papacy from the Byzantine Empire and to the conversion of the Frankish monarchy into the Holy Roman Empire. It abolished the national particularism of the territorial churches and restored the universalism of the Roman tradition. But it did so not by freeing the Church from secular control, but by the transformation of the territorial church into an imperial church and by a still more intimate fusion between the ecclesiastical and the territorial systems.

As we have seen, there were two fundamental elements in early mediaeval culture, the barbarian peoples and the Catholic Church. One found its organizing principle in the Germanic monarchies, the other in the Roman See. According to the ideas of Gregory the Great and St Boniface, these two powers should co-operate with one another for the conversion of Europe and the creation of a Christian order, an ideal which

[6] S. Boniface, *Ep.* 63.

was at least partially realized in Anglo-Saxon England during the seventh and eighth centuries and in the realm of the Franks during the co-operation of Boniface and Carloman. With the foundation of the Carolingian empire, however, the universal Church no longer had to deal with a number of local monarchies but with a single power which itself claimed to represent the principle of Christian universality and Roman order. The Catholic Church found its secular counterpart in the Holy Roman Empire, indeed something more than that, for the Carolingian state was itself a quasi-religious unity which asserted its sacred character and tended to regard the Church as nothing more than its theological and liturgical organ. The Carolingian Church was thus the state-church of a church-state. It had been freed from the worst abuses of the territorial system only because the secular power had become conscious of its ecclesiastical responsibilities and had itself acquired an almost ecclesiastical position. It was in fact the territorial church regularized and universalized to such a degree that the Papacy itself had been subordinated to its principles. Charlemagne was able to complete the Bonifacian reforms and to restore the canonical organization of metropolitans and provincial councils, because he himself now stood at the apex of the ecclesiastical pyramid, and the Pope was under his control.

But though the Carolingian system militated against the independence of the church and the effective supremacy of the Holy See, it nevertheless helped to strengthen both the Christian and Latin elements in Western culture. It created a new social unity in which the Germanic and Latin elements were combined organically instead of co-existing as two independent traditions, as had been the case in the earlier Germanic kingdoms. Here again the influence of monasticism was of the highest importance. The Carolingian abbeys were, apart from the royal palace, the only real centres of culture in the Empire. And their culture was almost entirely a Latin one, founded on the traditions of the Western fathers and the old schools of rhetoric, as transmitted through the influence of Cassiodorus and Columbanus and the monastic schools of England and Ireland.

Thus throughout the darkest period of the Middle Ages the Western Church preserved its intellectual tradition almost unimpaired, and the contemporaries of the Vikings possessed all and more than all of the patristic learning of the contemporaries of St Gregory. No doubt the monasteries were themselves exposed to the danger of secularization, but to nothing like the same extent as the rest of the Church. While the parish priest might be an ignorant peasant and the bishop a territorial magnate, who lived the same life as the secular nobility of his time, the monk, if he was to remain a monk at all, had to preserve his social and spiritual identity. The territorial church was a Christian hierarchy artificially superimposed on an alien social foundation and often almost absorbed by it, but the monastic society was Christian in its essential social constitution, and governed its whole life, at least in theory, not on the usages of its social environment but on the written law of the Benedictine rule. As Dom Ursmer Berlière has written, "The Benedictine abbey was a little state which could serve as model to the new Christian society which was arising from the fusion of conquered and conquering races, a state which had religion for its foundation, work restored to honour as its support, and a new intellectual and artistic culture as its crown."[7]

It is characteristic of mediaeval religion that its spiritual ideals found expression in a definite sociological organism. The spiritual life was not a vague aspiration, or an abstract idea, it was a *life* in the full sense of the word, an organized pattern of behaviour which was embodied in distinct institutional forms and which possessed an autonomous economic existence, which rendered it at least potentially independent of its social environment.

Thus whenever the territorial church tended to become a part of the machinery of the territorial state or to be overwhelmed by its barbaric environment, as occurred alike in the seventh and the tenth centuries, the monasteries preserved the principle of an autonomous Christian order which again and again proved to be the seed of new life for the whole Church. For the modern historian the great importance of monasticism may seem to lie in its services to culture, in its preservation of the tradition of letters and of classical literature. But from the point of view of mediaeval religion it is the essential monastic ideals of asceticism and otherworldliness and fidelity to the Rule that are the important matters, for it was these that gave it its spiritual independence, its power to resist the pressure of its environment and to initiate movements of reli-

[7] U. Berlière, *L'Ordre Monastique*, p. 41.

gious reform. That is why in the tenth century Cluny is of more importance than Reichenau or St Gall in spite of their greater culture and artistic activity, and why in the twelfth century Clairvaux is, in turn, more important than Cluny.

Now this monastic ideal of spiritual independence and of the strict observance of the Benedictine Rule had a natural affinity with the traditional Roman ideal of ecclesiastical independence under the sovereignty of the Papacy and of the strict observance of the canon law. As Dr Coulton writes, "(the monks) formed of all ecclesiastical bodies, that one whose general interests and ideals coincided most exactly with that of the papacy. They were truly a papal militia; *schola servitii* with a *lex sub qua militat*. What the military colonies were to the Roman Empire, the monasteries will now be to what we may call the papal empire."[8] And as Gregory the Great first called in the monks to help in the conversion of the new peoples and Gregory II and his successors allied himself with Boniface and the Anglo-Saxon monks for the conversion of Germany and the reform of the Frankish Church, so now Gregory VII allied himself with Cluny and with the monastic reformers of Lorraine and Italy in order to achieve his vast plan for a movement of universal reform and for the freeing of the Church from its bondage to the empire and the territorial system.

The struggle of the Investitures was an attempt to reverse the whole development of the territorial church from its roots in the rights of patronage and advowson and the lay proprietorship of ecclesiastical

[8] G. Coulton, *Five Centuries of Religion*, I, p. 217.

benefices (the principle of the *Eigenkirche*) to its consummation in the ecclesiastical imperialism of the Carolingian and Saxon emperors. It aimed, whether consciously or unconsciously, at undoing the work of Charlemagne, at cutting through the dense growth of custom and prescription that bound Church and state together and at reconstituting the Church as a free and universal spiritual society under the sovereignty of the Apostolic See with its own code of laws and its own independent legislative and judicial system.

Such a programme could only be realized on condition that the Church as a whole was animated by the same spirit of uncompromising unworldliness and ascetic fervour that characterized the movement of monastic reform. And to a considerable extent this was actually the case. The great reforming Popes—Leo IX, Gregory VII, Urban II, and many more—were themselves monks and found their allies and helpers among the leaders of the monastic reform or their disciples— St Peter Damian, Humbert of Moyenmoutier, Gerald of Ostia, Hugh of Cluny, St Anselm of Lucca and St Anselm of Canterbury. Moreover their work resulted in imparting to the mediaeval Church as a whole something of the monastic spirit, as we see above all in the enforcement of the celibacy of the clergy, which did so much to set apart the clergy as a separate body whose interests were bound up not with their family or their locality, but with the ecclesiastical order of which they formed part. The best of the mediaeval prelates, men such as Anselm, and Thomas of Canterbury, and Hugh of Lincoln—to quote examples from this country alone —were patterns of asceticism and of all the monastic virtues, and the fact that such men could hold the highest offices in the Church is enough to prove that the reforming movement was not without fruit.

Nevertheless, the full programme of the reformers was incapable of complete and immediate realization. It was impossible to reverse the whole development of the last five centuries by any changes, however revolutionary. It would have involved a fight to the death, not only with the State Church of the Empire, but with the whole feudal world of Western Europe. The only way in which it could have been achieved was through the solution which was accepted for a moment by the unworldly idealism of Pascal II in the Concordat of Sutri: that is to say by the Church's renunciation of all the endowments and privileges which it held of the secular power in return for the renunciation by the empire of its rights of investiture and control over ecclesiastical appointments—in other words, the separation of Church and State. Such a drastic solution, however, aroused the opposition of all the vested interests in the imperial church and was almost immediately abandoned by both parties. The solution that was actually reached by the Concordat of Worms was a compromise which left the roots of the problem untouched, a temporary truce which allowed the combatants to organize their forces before taking up the struggle again.

The conflict had, however, brought an immense gain of prestige to the Papacy and a corresponding loss to the Empire. Henceforward there was no question as to the international unity of the Church or the supreme authority of the Holy See. The Investiture controversy

was much more than a mere quarrel about ecclesiastical benefices, it involved new social principles and
ideals that transformed the whole character of European society. For the first time the unity of Christian
Europe, which had been implicit in the earlier mediaeval development, found explicit recognition in an international organization that was really effective and
genuinely international. The Holy Roman Empire,
especially in the age of Charlemagne, had, it is true,
attempted to realize this ideal, but it had failed owing
to the inherent weakness of the mediaeval state. The
Church and the Church alone possessed the power and
authority necessary to unite the semi-barbaric peoples
of Europe in a universal society. The mediaeval church
was not a group of individuals, united by common
religious opinions, like a modern sect; it was a true
kingdom with its own constitution and its own laws, it
embraced a much larger part of human life and im-
parted a far wider citizenship than did the fragmentary
and barbarous feudal state. It undertook far greater
social responsibilities, inasmuch as all that we now
think of as 'the social services', the care of the poor and
the sick, and the protection of the weak, belonged to
its province instead of to that of the state. Above all it
was the true organ of culture. Education, thought,
literature and art all existed primarily in and for the
Church, and it was the representative of the tradition of
Latin civilization and order, as well as of the Christian
ideals of charity and brotherhood.

Even in political matters the Papacy came to exercise
a kind of international authority, as the supreme court
of appeal and source of justice. It established a kind of

protectorate over the lesser kingdoms and the outlying territories of Christendom, as for example in Spain and Hungary, whose rulers took a special oath of allegiance to the Pope as 'Knights of St Peter' and vassals of the Holy See. And though this did not involve any direct political control, it emphasized the new position of the Papacy as the head of Christendom and the president of a sort of Christian league of nations.

Nevertheless these things were not the ends for which the reformers themselves had fought. Nothing could be more unhistorical than the traditional idea of Gregory VII as an ambitious ecclesiastical politician like Boniface VIII or Julius II. He was above all a reformer, and a champion of the spiritual freedom of the Church, and his ideals were fundamentally the same as those which St Augustine set forth in *The City of God*. He was inspired not, as a modern historian has said, by "magnificent visions of ecclesiastical grandeur" but by a profound sense of the degradation of the secularized Church of his age and the urgent need of reform.

"I cry, I cry and I cry again," he writes in his final appeal to the Christian world in 1084. "The religion of Christ, the true faith, has fallen so low that it is an object of scorn not only to the Devil, but to Jews and Saracens and pagans . . . These keep their law, as they believe it, but we, intoxicated with the love of the world, have deserted our law." "Every day we see thousands of men go to death for the sake of their lords, but if a few are found to resist, the wicked men do not help them but regard them as fools and madmen." "I have laboured with all my might that the Holy Church, the Bride of God, our mistress and our

mother, should recover her honour and remain chaste,
and free and Catholic."[9]

Thus the reforming movement was at once revolutionary and conservative. It broke with the tradition of
the Carolingian Empire and the territorial Church in
the name of canonical principles and of patristic and
apostolic ideals. But in the circumstances of the age,
this led to revolutionary innovations in the relation
between Church and State and to the active intervention
of the spiritual power in the social life of Christendom.
The distinction and independence of Church and State,
of the spiritual and temporal powers, was recognized
in theory as it had been in patristic times. But the con-
crete situation had been entirely changed by the territor-
ialization of the Church on the one hand, and by the
desecularization of the State on the other. In the patristic age, the Church, for all its power and privileges,
was a secondary society that existed in the Roman
Empire in the same way as the Church exists in the
modern state; as St Optatus writes, "The State is not in
the Church, but the Church is in the State, that is, in
the Roman Empire." But in the Middle Ages this
relation was reversed, and it could really be said that
the State was in the Church. The latter was the primary and fundamental social reality, and the state was
merely a subordinate institution charged with the
office of preserving peace and order. This conception,
which is of fundamental importance for the understanding of mediaeval ideas, is admirably stated by the
twelfth century canonist, Stephen of Tournai. "In the
same city and under the same king there are two peo-

[9] *Mon. Greg.* 572, etc.

ples, and corresponding to the two peoples two ways of life, corresponding to the two ways of life two authorities, and corresponding to the two authorities two orders of jurisdiction. The City is the Church, the King is Christ. The two peoples are the two orders in the Church, the clergy and the laity. The two ways of life are the spiritual and the carnal (or secular), the two authorities are the priesthood and the kingship, the two jurisdictions are the divine and human laws (canon and civil law). Give to each its due and all things will agree."[10]

This however was easier said than done. For the symmetry and completeness of mediaeval social theory was set off by the inextricable confusion of ecclesiastical and secular rights and jurisdictions that characterized the actual conditions of mediaeval society. The Holy Roman Empire was one attempt to achieve a synthesis, the Papal theocracy was another. Neither was completely successful. The ideal of Catholic universalism could not make the realities of the territorial system conform to strict canonical principles, while the territorial Church in spite of its centrifugal tendencies could not deny the validity of these principles or refuse allegiance to the universal ideals that were inherent in the Catholic tradition. This unresolved tension explains the ultimate disruption of mediaeval Christendom. Yet at the same time, it is an essential condition of the religious achievement of the Middle Ages. The Middle Ages were not the ages of Faith in the sense of unquestioning submission to authority and

[10] Carlyle, *History of Mediaeval Political Theory*, ii, p. 198 and iv, p. 166.

blind obedience. They were ages of spiritual struggle and social change, in which the existing situation was continually being modified by the reforming energy and the intellectual activity that were generated by the contact between the living stream of Christian tradition and the youthful peoples of the West.

RELIGION AND MEDIAEVAL CULTURE

II
THE THEOLOGICAL DEVELOPMENT

THE transformation which religion underwent in passing from the ancient to the mediaeval world was, as we have seen, mainly a sociological one. It was not accompanied by any revolutionary change in doctrine such as those that took place at the Reformation, or even those which marked the breaking away of the oriental Churches from the Church of the Empire. In matters of dogma mediaeval religion is characterized above all by its conservative spirit. It had inherited from the patristic age an enormous mass of theological learning, and its chief problem for centuries was how this learning was to be preserved and assimilated. Hence the impersonal note that marks the theological literature of the early middle ages. As Tixeront writes, "They did not believe that it was possible to renew or to advance the progress of doctrinal exposition, after the geniuses that had preceded them. They classify, they codify, they give their correspondents solutions and explanations; they hold councils for the reform of morals, but they remain rather on the surface of dogma. And one cannot be surprised when one considers the times in which they lived. It was no small thing in such an age and in such an environment merely to preserve the past and to instruct the terrible neophytes who were entering the Church in the elements of the catechism."[1]

Hence the student of mediaeval religion has constantly to be on his guard against confusing patristic and mediaeval thought. There are of course popular writers who do not attempt to make any distinction, and who are prepared to treat the whole development

[1] *Histoire des dogmes*, III, 324.

of Catholic thought from the age of Tertullian and Cyprian to that of Bossuet as mediaeval. But even scholars who fully realize the immense gulf that divides the ancient from the mediaeval world are often careless in this respect and describe ideas or beliefs as characteristic of the Middle Ages when they are in reality only the mediaeval echoes or repetitions of pure patristic tradition. Indeed the development of early mediaeval thought was so overshadowed by that of the patristic age that it is by no means easy to distinguish its original features. It is however important to remember that the expression 'Mediaeval Catholicism' is commonly used to describe three phases of religious development which are in point of time as far from one another as we ourselves are from the Reformation.

First, there is the religion of the later Roman Empire, which we may call Patristic Catholicism. Secondly there is the religion of the Dark Ages, the age of the conversion of the barbarians. Thirdly, there is the religion of the twelfth to the fourteenth centuries, which are often regarded as the central period of the Middle Ages but which were also, as Prof. Mandonnet and Prof. Haskins have pointed out, essentially an age of the renaissance of European culture.

Moreover we must also remember that in none of these periods was Catholicism or any form of Christianity the only European religion; in each of them it had rivals to contend with, and rivals which changed from age to age.

In the first age the ruling classes were still largely pagan and the Fathers of the Church had to meet the criticisms of highly educated men who despised

Christianity as an upstart oriental superstition that was a stranger to the glorious traditions of classical civilization, while at the same time they had to combat the attacks of numerous heretical sects, Arians, Donatists, Priscillianists and the rest, as well as the still more fundamental challenge of the Manichean dualism.

In the second age the scene has entirely changed. Heresy is practically non-existent in the West, the old educated paganism is dead, and the Church has herself become the representative of the traditions of classical culture in so far as they survive. But paganism is still strong, and threatens the Church, both from within and from without: from within, by the masses of uninstructed and half-converted peasants and barbarians who had found themselves Christians, as it were without knowing it, owing to the conversion of their landlords and chieftains; from without, by the warrior peoples of the North and the East, whose attacks again and again threatened to destroy the new Christian culture that had been painfully and laboriously built up in the West.

Finally in the third age, Catholicism has emerged victorious, and the Church has become the mistress and teacher of Western society. Nevertheless, her position is not uncontested. The revival of trade and town life was accompanied by a new current of Manichean influence from the East through the Balkan peninsula; while the movement for ecclesiastical reform, in spite of its fundamental orthodoxy, contained explosive elements which sometimes attained an unorthodox and revolutionary character, as, for example, with

the Waldenses and the Franciscan Spirituals. Moreover, the expansion of Christendom brought the
Church into contact and conflict with the thought of
the modern world, which in the twelfth century still
possessed a strong centre of diffusion in south-western
Europe. Indeed, the most influential European thinker
of the age was not a Christian, but the Spanish Moslem,
Averroes. Thus once more, as in the patristic age, the
representatives of Christian thought had to meet the
criticism of highly educated antagonists who were
their equals or even their superiors in philosophic and
scientific equipment. In fact, it was not until the second
half of the thirtenth century that Western Christendom
had attained a sufficiently high level of culture to meet
the modern philosophers on their own ground.

In this extended sense the history of mediaeval culture covers a thousand years and throughout that
period the development of Catholic thought was characterized by a remarkable unity and continuity.

In each of the three phases of this development,
however, Catholic theology possesses distinctive features that are determined by the conditions I have just
referred to. The patristic age was the creative period of
western theology and finds its fullest expression in the
personality and work of St Augustine. The second age
was the age of traditionalism *par excellence*, and its typical representatives are Gregory the Great and the
Venerable Bede; while the third age was the age of
scholasticism—of the systematic dialectical reorganization of the whole traditional material—a work
which was begun by Anselm and Abelard and Peter
Lombard and which achieved complete expression in

the great philosophical synthesis of St Thomas Aquinas. It is possible to say without exaggeration that whatever was given in the first phase of this development was
preserved in the second and was incorporated into the
organic unity of scholastic theology in the third. Nothing was lost. All the materials that lie scattered in the
writings of the Fathers—in sermons and commentaries
and controversial treatises—are to be found again built
up into the imposing and symmetrical edifice of
thirteenth century scholastic theology.

II

THIS organic development was however a process
that was limited by the frontiers of the Latin-Christian
culture and the Western tradition. It did not include
Greek-Christian culture and the tradition of the Eastern Church except in so far as these were already incorporated in the teaching of the Latin fathers.
Throughout the middle ages East and West followed a
separate line of theological development, and this goes
far to explain the division of the Churches and the growing alienation of the Eastern and Western minds. From
the first the theological interests of the two halves of
Christendom had been different, and while the Christian East was passionately absorbed in the great Chris-
tological controversies that tore the Byzantine Church
and Empire asunder, the West was far more interested
in questions of ecclesiastical order and moral discipline
such as those which gave rise to the Novatian and
Donatist heresies. It was not until the time of the Pela-

gian controversy that a theological issue of the first
importance arose in the West, and even here the centre
of interest was predominantly moral in comparison
with the speculative metaphysical problems that absorbed the Greek mind.

These interests continued to characterize the theological development of the Eastern and Western Churches. Theology in the West found its centre and principle of organization in the doctrine of Grace; the
sacraments are conceived primarily as Means of Grace,
and the Christian life is the Life of Grace. In the East
theology is the doctrine of the Consubstantial Word.
The sacraments are conceived as mysteries of illumination, and .the Christian life is seen as a process of
deification by which humanity is assimilated to the
immortal nature of the Divine Word. Thus the tendency of Western theology finds its representative and
embodiment in St Augustine, the Doctor of Grace,
whose influence dominates the whole mediaeval
development, while the typical representative of Eastern theology is to be found in Origen who continued
to influence the development of Greek Christian
thought through the medium of Athanasius and the
great Cappadocian Fathers, Basil and the two Gregor-
ies. There is however a striking difference in the fortunes of these two great names, for while St Augustine
remained and still remains the acknowledged Father of
Western theology, Origen was disowned and abandoned by his spiritual descendants and his writings
were proscribed as heretical. Indeed by a strange para-
dox, the writings of the greatest of the Greek Fathers
survive to a great extent only in Latin translations and

in Western MSS which are incomparably more numerous than the Greek MSS of those parts of the original
text of his writings that still remain. This points to an
aspect of mediaeval western culture which is seldom
sufficiently recognized—namely its openmindedness,
and its readiness to incorporate foreign elements in its
intellectual tradition. For while the Orthodox East
was too proud of its high culture and its wealth of
theological learning to learn anything from the West,[2]
the Latin world remained open to oriental influences
and was fertilized by intellectual and spiritual elements
drawn from outside.

This is to be seen not only in the wholesale translation and adaptation of Greek theological works which
marked the patristic age itself, the age of Rufinus and
Jerome, and Marius Victorinus, of Hilary and Ambrose,
but also in later periods. Even the Dark Ages did not
pass without some fresh additions to the intellectual
patrimony of the West, notably the translations of the
works of the Pseudo-Dionysius, which were of epoch-
making importance in the development of the religious
thought of the middle ages. Finally in the third period
the new developments in Western theology and the
immense progress realized by the scholastic movement
are closely connected with a new stream of oriental influences, due to the mass of new material brought into
the Latin world by the translators of the twelfth and
thirteenth centuries. The greater part of this material

[2] The first important translations from Latin into Greek were
made by Maximus Planudes who translated Boethius, St
Augustine on the Trinity and perhaps also the *Summa Theologica*
of St Thomas, about the end of the thirteenth century.

was scientific and philosophical, but in addition to this main stream of Aristotelian and Arabic influence there were also a number of translations of the works of the Greek Fathers which had a direct influence on Western theology.

The most important of these was the treatise of St John Damascene on The Orthodox Faith, the third part of his great theological summa, *The Source of Knowledge*, which is a systematic and authoritative summary of the whole Greek theological tradition. This work was first translated into Latin by Burgundio of Pisa in the middle of the twelfth century and almost immediately, in spite of the attacks of a few bigoted traditionalists, became one of the standard authorities of Western theology, owing to its partial utilization by Peter Lombard in his *Sentences*. It was translated yet again by Robert Grosseteste in the thirteenth century and was used extensively by St Thomas and the other great scholastics.

This work, together with other translations from the Greek, above all the Pseudo-Dionysian writings with the comment of St Maximus which were translated again and again during the middle ages, had an important effect on Western theology. It led the scholastics—above all St Bonaventure and St Thomas—to revise and complete the Augustinian doctrine of grace in the light of the teaching of the Greek fathers and thus to create a synthesis of the two great theological traditions of the East and the West. While preserving the broad lines of the Augustinian doctrine, they laid a much greater emphasis on the ontological character of the supernatural order. While Augustine conceives

grace primarily as an act of divine power that moves
the human will, Thomas considers it above all under
its essential aspect of the new spiritual principle which
transforms and renews human nature by the communication of the Divine Life: in other words the state of
deification of which the Greek fathers habitually
speak. It is not merely a power that moves the will but
a *light* that illuminates the mind and transfigures the
whole spirit. This combination of the Augustinian
tradition with the characteristic doctrine of the Greek
Fathers is perhaps the greatest theological achievement
of the scholastic period, though it is usually little
noticed in comparison with their philosophical synthesis. Although it was not always fully accepted or
fully understood by the later scholastics, it became the
basis of classical Catholic theology, and when the
great theological struggle of the Reformation came, it
was at once the centre of the Protestant attack and the
rallying point of the Catholic defence.

III

MOREOVER the influence of Greek religious thought
was not confined to the theological schools and to the
learned tradition, it had a direct influence on the religious life of the West, owing to the rise of the new
schools of mysticism which were intimately connected
with the scholastic development. These owed even
more than scholasticism in general to the new elements
of Byzantine thought imported into the West by the
works of the Pseudo-Dionysius and by other Neopla-

tonic treatises such as the *Liber de Causis,* and the *Introduction to Theology* of Proclus, which last was translated by William of Moerbeke, the Flemish Archbishop of Corinth and the friend of St Thomas. Mysticism was no new religious phenomenon in mediaeval Europe. The Neoplatonic influences which reached the West in an undiluted form in the thirteenth century, were already present from the beginning in Marius Victorinus and Macrobius and Boethius and above all in St Augustine himself. The latter united his Neoplatonic doctrine of contemplation and illumination with a highly individual and essentially Christian mysticism of dynamic charity which became the characteristic note of Western mysticism, in the same way as the closely allied Augustinian doctrine of grace became characteristic of Western theology as a whole.

As Abbot Butler has shown in his work on Western Mysticism, this Augustinian mystical tradition is carried on by St Gregory and St Bernard, the two most influential spiritual writers of their respective periods, and dominates the spiritual life of the Western Church down to the age of scholasticism.

The mysticism of St Augustine is intensely personal and possesses a psychological and introspective character that is lacking, or at least extremely rare, in the mysticism of the Christian East. In this respect it is very significant that the great mystical classic of the Eastern Church should be the work of an unknown author who hides his personality under the name of the Areopagite, while the fountain head of Western mysticism should be the great spiritual autobiography in which St Augustine makes his own inner life the key to the deep things of God. And these divergent tendencies continued to distinguish the spirituality of the Eastern and Western Church. Eastern mysticism remained impersonal and never expressed itself in religious auto-biography or self-revelation, save possibly in Russia during recent centuries, while in the West, from the time of St Augustine to our own days, spirituality has always tended to possess a highly individual and personal character, and spiritual autobiographies have been the classics of Western mysticism.

But while the mysticism of St Augustine is one of the most fundamental and permanent elements in the religious tradition of the West, its influence reached its climax in the twelfth century before the coming of the oriental influences to which I have just referred. The twelfth century was a period of immense spiritual and cultural vitality. It has been called the age of the mediae-val renaissance, but it was a renaissance that was not only intellectual, but also religious. If it produced hum-anists like John of Salisbury, philosophers like Abelard and Bernard of Tours, and poets like Chrétien of Troyes, its greatest, and, on the whole, its most re-presentative figure was an ascetic and mystic, St Bern-ard of Clairvaux, the last of the Fathers.

The mysticism of St Bernard and the whole Cister-cian school, above all that of his friend and disciple, William of St Thierry, is profoundly Augustinian. It is, like St Augustine's, a mysticism of charity—*theolo-gia cordis*— but to an even greater degree, since with St Bernard the affective and voluntarist element complete-ly overcomes the Neoplatonic intellectualism which still retained its influence over St Augustine's mind. To

St Bernard love is better than knowledge, since it reaches beyond knowledge and is its own cause and end. "*Amor praeter se non requirit causam, non fructum. Fructus ejus, usus ejus. Amo quia amo; amo ut amem. Magna res amor, si tamen ad suum recurrat principium, si suae origini redditus, si refusus suo fonti, semper ex eo sumat unde jugiter fluat. Solus est amor ex omnibus animae motibus, sensibus atque affectibus in quo potest creatura, etsi non ex aequo, respondere auctori vel de simili mutuam rependere vicem.*"[3]

This is the theme of St Bernard's sermons on the Canticles, which is one of the classics of mediaeval religious literature, and which had an immense influence on the development of Western mysticism. The allegorical interpretation of Canticles as an epithalamium on the mystical marriage between the human soul and the Divine Word, has its roots deep in the tradition of the Eastern Church with Origen and Methodius of Olympus, and Gregory of Nyssa. But it was through St Bernard that it first became completely incorporated in the Western spiritual tradition, passing on through Richard of St Victor and St Bonaventure to St John of the Cross and the mystics of the seventeenth century, both Catholic and Protestant. This is one of the aspects of mediaeval spirituality that is least sympathetic to

[3] *In Cantica*, LXXXIII, 4. "Love seeks no cause nor end but itself. Its fruit is its activity. I love because I love, I love that I may love. Love is a mighty thing, if so it returns to its own principle and origin, if it flows back to its source and ever draws anew whence it may flow again. Love is the only one of all the senses, movements and affections of the soul, by which the creature can answer to its creator and repay like with like."

the modern mind, which is apt to regard the mystical
Eros as a perversion of, or a substitute for, sexual passion. But the mediaeval Christian, whether philosopher
or mystic, viewed the matter from a diametrically opposite point of view. To him, divine love was the reality and human love the shadow. The cosmic process
has its origin in the overflowing of the love of God
which is the act of creation and finds its motive force
in the desire by which all creation seeks to return to its
source. And hence sexual passion is but a blind and perverted form of the universal force which finds its true,
conscious and normal expression in the love of God.

This philosophy of love, which is implicit in the
whole thought and life of St Bernard, had been developed in its full metaphysical implications by the Pseudo-
Areopagite in his treatise on the Divine Names.

"By all things," he writes, "is the Beautiful and the
Good, desired and loved and chosen to be loved; and because of it and for its sake those that are lower love
those that are higher by attraction, and those that are
of the same rank love their equals in communion, and
the higher love the lower by forethought and kindness,
and each loves its own by coherence; and all things by
desiring the Beautiful and Good do and will whatso-
ever they do and will. Further it may be truly said that
the very Cause of all things, by reason of the overflow
of His Goodness, loves all, creates all, perfects all, holds
all together, turns all to Himself; and the Divine Love
is the Good and of the Good and by reason of the Good.
For that Love itself, working the good of existing
things, pre-existing overflowingly in the Good, did

not suffer Him to remain in Himself without Fruit, but moved Him to creation, by the overflowing which is generative of all things."

"And let us not be afraid of this name of Love (Eros) or be perturbed by what anyone may say against it. For the theologians seem to me to treat the words Charity and Love (Agape and Eros) as equivalent, and preferred to reserve love in the absolute sense for divine things, on account of the misplaced prejudice of the vulgar. For though Love in Itself is spoken of in the, divine sense not by us only, but by the Oracles [the Scriptures] themselves, the multitude, not comprehending the oneness of the divine name of Love, fell away, as might be expected of them, to a divided, material, and partial conception of love, which is not true love, but a shadow of Love itself, or rather a falling away from it."[4]

Thus the devotional mysticism of St Bernard and his school, especially William of St Thierry, finds its philosophical complement in the mystical metaphysics of the Pseudo-Areopagite, and it was the union of these two traditions which gave birth to the great development of speculative mysticism in the later middle ages. The earliest contact between the two traditions took place in the twelfth century with Hugh and Richard of St Victor. It is true that the works of the Pseudo-Areopagite had been accessible in the West ever since the ninth century, when they were first translated by Hilduin of St Denys. But apart from the outstanding exception of John Scotus Erigena, whose mystical Neoplatonism had singularly little influence either on his contemporaries or his successors, the Dionysian writ-

[4] *The Divine Names*, IV, 10, 12.

ings had no real importance for Western thought until the sudden awakening of interest in the twelfth century which shows itself in the successive commentaries on the book of the Celestial Hierarchies, produced by Hervé of Deols, 1110-130, by Hugh of St Victor about 1137, and by John Sarrazin who died in 1180. But even in the case of Hugh of St Victor the Dionysian influence is slight, and on the whole the Victorine school belongs to the same Western Augustinian tradition as the Cistercian school with which they are so closely allied, until we come to the time of Thomas of St Victor, afterwards Abbot of Vercelli, about 1225, who fused the tradition of the school of St Victor with the teachings of the Pseudo-Dionysius, which he did so much to popularize by his translations and adaptations.

It was, however, among the great scholastics of the thirteenth century that the influence of the Pseudo-Dionysius and the Neoplatonists attains its complete development. Indeed, so far from scholasticism and mysticism being two hostile and contradictory forces in mediaeval thought, we may justly describe the introspective mysticism of the later middle ages, especially the school of Eckhart, Tauler and Ruysbroeck as 'scholastic mysticism', since it is as closely bound up with the scholastic development of the thirteenth and fourteenth centuries as is Thomism itself. In fact, these two movements had a common source in the teaching of St Albert the Great, who was the teacher both of St Thomas on the one hand and of Ulrich of Strasburg on the other, from whom in turn the tradition was handed on through Dietrich of Freiberg to Eckhart who was universally acknowledged as the founder and master

of the great school of fourteenth-century German and
Flemish mysticism. No doubt it is possible to contrast
the Neoplatonism of this school with the Aristotelianism of St Thomas, so as to make them appear completely opposed to one another. But we must remember
that the Aristotelianism of St Thomas was profoundly
impregnated with Neoplatonic elements, and that the
Dionysian writings were themselves one of the main
formative influences on St Thomas's thought, while on
the other hand Eckhart and Tauler and the rest were
themselves students of Aristotle and St Thomas, and
regarded the latter as the great theologian of their
order.[5]

In Eckhart the Dionysian current, reinforced by further Neoplatonic elements derived from Proclus and
the Arabs, reaches its extreme development and seems
to pass the utmost bounds of orthodoxy and to bring
the mediaeval theological development to a conclusion
not far removed from the pure monism of the Vedanta.
Nevertheless, as Denifle pointed out long ago, Eckhart
is not an oriental pantheist nor a modern idealist, he is
a mediaeval Dominican and a scholastic, and in order to
understand his views it is necessary to put them in their
historical context and relate them to the intellectual
milieu in which they originated. Thus when Eckhart
asserts that God is all, that creatures are sheer nothing
and that it is a fallacy to speak of God as good, he is
merely expressing in paradoxical and unguarded language the commonplaces of the Dionysian theology
which are to be found in a more balanced but no less

[5] Cf. G. Théry in his *Introduction Historique* to Tauler's Sermons, tr. Hugueny, vol. I, 192-7.

complete form in the standard works of Ulrich of Strasburg and of St Thomas himself.

But whatever may be thought of Eckhart, there can be no question as to the fundamental and entire orthodoxy of his disciples, John Tauler, Henry Suso, Henry of Nordlingen, and John Ruysbroeck, through whom the mystical metaphysics of Pseudo-Dionysius and Eckhart became one of the great sources of spiritual life and inspiration for the later mediaeval church. The Friends of God, as they were called, gained adherents among every class throughout the Rhineland and Lower Germany. They included not only learned Dominican theologians, like Tauler, and nuns like the members of the Dominican communities at Töss and Unterlinden, but also secular priests, like Henry of Nordlingen, knights of the Teutonic Order such as Nicholas von Laufen, the Strasburg banker Rulman Merswin, and even peasants and uneducated lay people. Thus the *via negativa* of the mediaeval mystic, which seems to the outsider to lead to a pantheistic nihilism that leaves no room for any social or moral activity, actually inspired one of the great popular religious movements of the Middle Ages.

It is a striking example—perhaps the most striking instance in history—of the way in which abstract theological thought may affect religious life and social action, and it is the more remarkable when we consider how unfavourable were the circumstances of the time and place for the development of such a highly intellectualized and esoteric type of religion.

IV

BUT while this mystical movement represents one of the peaks of the mediaeval religious development, it was by no means the only or the most important one. The movement which had the greatest influence on mediaeval religion and mediaeval culture was not the speculative mysticism of the Dominicans, but the evangelical piety and the devotion to the Humanity of Jesus that found its supreme expression in the life of St Francis. This movement has far less connection with the scientific theology of the schools than the other, though one of its most notable representatives, St Bonaventure, was also one of the greatest of scholastic theologians. It was preeminently practical, emotional and human, owing nothing to learned tradition or metaphysical ideas, but springing directly from the heart and from personal experience. The greatest religious achievement of the Middle Ages is not to be found in the imposing edifice of its ecclesiastical organization, or in its work of intellectual synthesis, but in its deepening of the spiritual life by a new type of religious experience which had a profound influence on Western Christianity.

One of the most original and suggestive of modern writers on mediaeval religion, the late Pierre Rousselot, has written of this change as follows: "St Augustine had considered the struggle for truth and holiness, before all, as a personal affair between the individual soul and God; it is by that that he had so to speak 'interiorized God'. But he had not in the same way interiorized Jesus. The humanity of Christ remains with him rather in the background. The great novelty of the Middle Ages, their incomparable religious merit, was the understanding and love, or rather one may say, the passion of the humanity of Christ. The Incarnate Word, *homo Christus Jesus*, is no longer only the model to be imitated, the guide to be followed, and on the other hand, the uncreated light that enlightens the interior of the soul; he is interior, even in respect of His Humanity; He is the *spouse* of the soul, who acts with it and in it; He is the friend."[6]

Now this new development of the religious tradition of the West, this new type of Christian sensibility, had already made its appearance in the early twelfth century with St Bernard. In his teaching the Humanity of Jesus acquires a new significance. In place of the severe figure of the Byzantine Christ, throned in awful majesty as the ruler and judge of men, St Bernard prefers to dwell on the human likeness of Jesus, the human suffering of His Passion and the human weakness of His Infancy. "*Arbitror Jesum et Joseph, virum Mariae, super genua frequenter arrisisse,*"[7] he writes, and again: "O man, why do you dread the face of the Lord? . . . Say not, like Adam, 'I heard His Voice and I hid me,' for behold He is a speechless infant, and the voice of a child crying is more to be pitied than feared."[8]

This was a new note in Christian literature and one which was to be repeated in countless meditations and hymns, such as the famous *Jesus dulcis memoria* and the

[6] *Christus* ed. V. Huby (1916), pp. 1119-1120.
[7] *In Cantica*, XLIII, 5.
[8] *Serm. in Nat. Dom.* I, 3.

Salve caput cruentatum. Nor is their influence confined to the Catholic world, it was also the principal inspiration of the Moravian and Methodist hymn writers and of their Christocentric piety. And all this tradition has its source in St Bernard and his disciples, above all the English Cistercians, such as Aelred of Rievaulx, the author of the little treatise *On Jesus a boy of twelve years old,* Isaac of Stella, Gilbert of Hoyland, and Stephen of Sawley.

But it was in St Francis of Assisi that this new spiritual culture bore its final and most perfect fruit. He is the embodiment in flesh and blood of the new spirit of Western Christianity. Hitherto though Christianity had been the great formative power in Western culture, it had been a foreign power that was still, as it were, something external to the nature of Western man, its real centres of life were in the monasteries, those camps of the disciplined *militia Dei,* which were scattered over the half pagan soil of Europe like fortresses in a newly conquered territory. With St Francis, for the first time we see Christianity breaking through the barriers of race and social tradition and achieving an organic and complete expression in Western man. There is no longer any conflict or inconsistency between religion and culture, between faith and life. The whole man is Christian, and the Christian spirit is united with the Western nature as intimately and inseparably as the union of soul and body.

Nothing could be more spontaneous, less artificial and 'cultured' than the genius of St Francis, yet he is the final fruit of a long process of spiritual cultivation. He marks the coming of age of Christian Europe and the birth of a new consciousness. And hence it is no accident that his advent should have been followed by the appearance of a new Christian art and poetry which, as Walter Pater wrote, "gave visible feature and colour and a palpable place among men to the regenerate race."

V

IT is true that this European Renaissance failed to fulfil the spiritual promise of its beginnings, just as the Byzantine culture failed to justify the promise of the earlier Christian centuries. The fourteenth century was an age of deception and disappointment, the age of the Black Death, and the Great Schism, and the Hundred Years' War. It saw the partial disruption of the unity of Christendom and the decline of that movement of spiritual reform which had been the soul of mediaeval culture. From the tenth to the thirteenth century the movement of European culture under the urge of a powerful religious impulse had been centripetal, towards unity and towards the ideals of Catholic universalism. From the beginning of the fourteenth century this tendency is reversed and a centrifugal movement sets in which ultimately culminates in the Reformation and the complete destruction of the religious unity of Christendom. The territorial element in the Church once more reasserted itself as opposed to the tradition of Catholic universalism, whose claims now seemed irreconcilable with the prerogatives of the new national monarchies.

The causes of this change are complex and obscure,

since they involve a number of both sociological and religious factors. On the one hand, the renaissance of Western civilization itself strengthened the centrifugal tendency by the new life that it brought to the national cultures. In the early middle ages, the nations had been the *gentes*, the descendants of the barbarian tribes that had invaded the empire, while the Church represented the traditions of Roman order and higher civilization. But now this duality of culture had been overcome and the peoples of the West were full of the pride of youth and the consciousness of their latent powers. The state was no longer a confused tangle of feudal and regional units engaged in perpetual war. It had achieved political order, and in the Western kingdoms at least, national unity. And consequently when they had overcome the anarchy and separation of feudalism, they felt that the Church, with its international system of jurisdiction and finance and its vast territorial endowments, was a rival that interfered with the full realization of their ideals of sovereignty and autonomy.

But on the other hand this nationalist tendency was reinforced by influences of a purely religious character. In the earlier conflicts between Church and State, Rome stood for the cause of ecclesiastical reform and spiritual freedom, and the great spiritual reformers, Humbert of Moyenmoutier, Peter Damien, St Anselm, St Bernard, St Francis and St Dominic, were the champions of the Papacy. In the fourteenth century, however, this was no longer the case. The defeat of the Papacy in its first great conflict with the national monarchy, represented by Philip the Fair, had led to its removal from Rome to Avignon, an event which did more than anything else to destroy its supernational prestige. The result was that the reformers themselves began to abandon the cause of the Papacy, and to look for help either to the secular power, as did Dante, and William of Ockam, and the spiritual Franciscans, or, like Gerson and d'Ailly and Langenstein, to the territorial Church and to the ecclesiastical parliamentarism of the Council of Constance, which in Dr Figgis' phrase "attempted to turn into a tepid constitutionalism the Divine authority of a thousand years."[9]

Finally in the Hussite movement we see the reforming spirit separating itself altogether from the Catholic tradition and coalescing with the spirit of nationalism to produce a great explosion of revolutionary feeling, which already betokens the end of the mediaeval order.

Thus the breach between the Papacy and the spiritual reformers is the vital cause of the decline of the mediaeval Church and is one of the main factors in the dissolution of the mediaeval unity and the transformation that passed over Europe in the later Middle Ages. We can trace its influence in later mediaeval poetry, in Dante, and Petrarch and Langland, no less than in theological literature proper. But its earliest manifestation is to be found in the extreme wing of the Franciscan order, the followers of John Peter Olivi and Angelo Clareno, and the disruption of the Franciscan movement is the first symptom of the approaching disruption of mediaeval Christendom. If the Franciscan movement had fulfilled the promise of its beginnings, it might have played the same part in the later mediaeval Church as the monastic reformers had done in the

[9] *Gerson to Grotius*, p. 35.

Church of the eleventh and twelfth centuries. Actually we see the beginnings of such a development in the missionary activity of the Friars, both in Europe and Asia, and in the part that they took in the university movement and in the life of the mediaeval city. Never, in fact, had the prospects of Christendom seemed more hopeful or its spiritual ideals nearer to their realization than in the thirteenth century. Men believed that they were on the threshold of great events, and they saw in St Francis the herald of a new age. The extreme form of this apocalyptic tendency is represented by the followers of Joachim of Flora, who announced the coming of the third kingdom and the Eternal Gospel. But it was by no means confined to them. It finds expression in most of the great minds of the age, in St Bonaventure and Mechtild of Magdeburg, in Roger Bacon and Ramon Lull and Dante. Thus St Bonaventure, who was no Joachimist, but rather the representative of the opposite tendency in the Order, regards St Francis as the type of the new seraphic order of spiritual men, and as the herald of the time "when the city of God will be built up and restored as it was in the beginning in the likeness of the Heavenly City and when the reign of peace will come."[10]

And when St Bonaventure died he may well have believed that his hopes were about to be realized, for the moment of his death coincided with a last triumph of the ideals of Catholic universalism and spiritual reform. Gregory X, perhaps the best, if not the greatest of the thirteenth-century Popes, had dedicated himself to the cause of peace. He had broken with Charles of

[10] *In Hexaemeron*, XVI, 30.

Anjou, the evil genius of the Papacy, and had ended the long feud with the Empire, and he now summoned the greatest of all the mediaeval councils to Lyons in 1274 to restore the unity of Christendom by the extinction of the still older schism with the Greek Church and to carry on the work of ecclesiastical reform with the help of the greatest thinkers of the age. St Thomas, it is true, died on his way to the Council, while St Bonaventure himself died during its session, but he could say his *Nunc dimittis*, for he had taken part in the final negotiations with the ambassador of the Byzantine Emperor, and had preached at the bi-lingual Mass which celebrated the reunion of East and West.

Nor were the Greeks the only orientals to be present at the Council. Its cosmopolitan importance was marked by the presence of an embassy from Abagha, the Khan of the Tartars, who had been sent to conclude an alliance with the Christians against the Sultan of Egypt, the last independent Moslem ruler. It seemed as though the power of Islam which had threatened the very existence of Christendom for so many centuries, was itself destined to destruction and that Asia would once more be thrown open to Christianity. Indeed, thanks to the favour of the Mongol princes, it was possible for the Franciscan, John of Montecorvino, to visit the Far East and to found missions and bishoprics in India and China.

Nevertheless, the promise of a new age of Christian unity and progress was doomed to disappointment. The Council of Lyons marks an end, not a beginning. In thirty years all these brilliant prospects were ruined. The union of the churches had vanished with the death of the emperor who had procured it. The last remnant of Christian dominion in Palestine had disappeared, and the Mongol rulers of Persia instead of destroying Islam had themselves become Moslems. The spiritual inspiration of the Franciscan movement had become obscured by the sterile controversies between the parties of the stricter and the laxer observance. Finally the Papacy itself had suffered a tremendous defeat at the hands of the French monarchy and was about to go into exile at Avignon, thus forfeiting the traditional prestige that had made Rome for so many centuries the spiritual capital of the Christian world. Thus the thirteenth century, for all its great religious achievement and its brilliant cultural development, proved fatal to the ideal of spiritual unity that was the centre of the mediaeval religious development. The age of St Francis and St Louis became the age of Boniface VIII and Philip the Fair. Men felt, with Dante, that they had lost a great opportunity and had made a great refusal, but they were no longer able to find a rallying point that would unite them in the common cause. Hence though the fourteenth century was an intensely religious age, it was no longer spiritually constructive. It was essentially an age of transition in which the new forces that were to destroy the mediaeval order were already active.

RELIGION AND MEDIAEVAL CULTURE

III
RELIGION AND MEDIAEVAL SCIENCE

1

THE ultimate criterion by which we must judge the value of a religion is not its cultural fruits but its spiritual truth. This, however, is not the criterion which the historian or the sociologist applies in his judgment of an age or a civilization. A false religion which produces a great art or a great literature— a religion which expresses itself in a brilliant civilization —will naturally be of greater interest to him than a true religion which produces only martyrs or mystics. But while the historian is justified in judging the cultural value of a religion by its cultural fruits, he has no right to treat his conclusions as final from the religious point of view. Actually however it is very difficult for an historian to preserve this distinction between religious and cultural values. If he believes a religion to be true, he will naturally tend to take a favourable view of the culture with which it is associated, and if he regards a culture as barbarous or unprogressive, he will be apt to condemn or depreciate its religious standards and beliefs.

Now it was on this ground that the traditional humanistic criticism of mediaeval religion was based. Mediaeval literature, mediaeval philosophy and mediaeval science alike appeared beneath contempt in the eyes of the Renaissance scholar, and still more of the philosopher of the eighteenth-century Enlightenment, and consequently mediaeval religion either shared in their condemnation or, still more frequently, was regarded as primarily responsible for the cultural backwardness of mediaeval Europe—in Gibbon's famous phrase, the Middle Ages were "the triumph of barbarism and religion."

This wholesale condemnation of mediaeval culture has long since been abandoned by the educated world, and it was the rediscovery of the purely cultural values of the Middle Ages—of mediaeval literature and mediaeval art—which was the main factor in bringing about the change, and which contributed very materially to a wider appreciation of the value of mediaeval religion. The rediscovery of mediaeval thought came later and was far less general. It was mainly confined to those who were already convinced of the religious values of mediaeval culture, and it was slow to affect public opinion generally. Nevertheless, it has not been without its effect and to-day there are few historians of philosophy who do not recognize the greatness of mediaeval intellectual achievement. It is true that so distinguished an historian as the late J. B. Bury could still describe mediaeval thought under the rubric 'Reason in Prison', but the book in question was written with a pronounced rationalistic bias, and as a rule even those who regard mediaeval metaphysics as of purely historical interest, nevertheless recognize, like Prof. Whitehead, that the European mind received from mediaeval scholasticism that fundamental training in rational thought on which all its later achievements are dependent.

But when we come to the question of natural science the old view still holds the field to a great extent, in spite of the work accomplished in recent years by writers such as the late Pierre Duhem and Dr George Sarton. To the scientist the Middle Ages are still the Dark Ages, and mediaeval religion is still regarded as an obscurantist force which set back and retarded the development of scientific thought.

Now it must be admitted that the Middle Ages witnessed a great decline in scientific knowledge from the standards already attained in the Greek world, and that there is a good *prima facie* case for ascribing this decline to the advent of Christianity and to the consequent turning away of men's attention from this world to the next and from the facts of Nature to the truths of faith. Does not St Augustine, the Patriarch of Western Christian thought, speak of science as a vain curiosity that distracts the mind from its true end, which is not to number the stars and to seek out the hidden things of nature, but to know and love God? Did not the monks murder Hypatia? and did not Justinian close the schools of Athens which still kept the sparks of Greek science and philosophy alive?

All this is true enough; nevertheless it is necessary to remember that the issue is not such a simple one as appears at first sight. The science of which St Augustine speaks was the science of astrology, which in our eyes is no science at all, though to the men of that age it seemed inseparable from what we call astronomy; and in the same way the school of Athens in spite of its genuine devotion to Hellenic science was inspired by a belief in occultism and magic that is far more fatal to the scientific ideal than the theology and the theological philosophy of Augustine; while as to the murder ot Hypatia, that had no more to do with her scientific accomplishments than the exile of Einstein from Germany has to do with Relativity. The fact is that the decline of ancient science is but one aspect of the vital decay of Hellenic culture, and when Christianity conquered ancient civilization, it occupied a house that was already empty. The life had gone out of it, and a new spirit was to take its place.

But if this is so, how are we to explain the backwardness of the Christian West in comparison with the Moslem East? It was the Arabs not the Christians who entered into the inheritance of Hellenic science and carried on its work, and throughout the early mediaeval centuries, while the West was completely barren of scientific achievement, the Moslem world, from Spain to Afghanistan, was the scene of an intense intellectual activity which showed itself not only in philosophy but in mathematics and astronomy and medicine.

The contrast is a very striking one, but it is impossible to explain it on religious grounds. For religion dominated Moslem culture no less than that of Christendom and Moslem theology was even more exclusive and universal in its claims than that of the Catholic Church. The causes of the difference were material rather than spiritual and are to be found primarily in the economic and social backwardness of the simple agrarian culture of Western Europe in comparison with the rich urban civilization of the Eastern Khalifate.

But in addition to this, there is a further historical factor that is of prime importance. Moslem culture entered into direct relations with Hellenism and was able to draw on the rich resources of Greek literature. The new peoples of the West, on the other hand, were tributary to Latin culture, and only possessed an indirect and secondary contact with the Hellenic tradition. And while Latin culture had been schooled in the classical traditions of Hellenic literature, it had never fully assimilated the Greek scientific tradition. Consequently where the Arabs could draw on the accumulated riches of the Aristotelian tradition, of Ptolemy and the earlier astronomers and the Greek mathematicians, the West had to content itself with the work of cultivated amateurs like Pliny, and the elementary notions of Greek philosophy transmitted by such writers as Boethius, Cassiodorus, Marius Victorinus, Macrobius, and Apuleius. The responsibility for this state of things rests not on the Church nor on mediaeval culture but on the secular culture of the Roman Empire which had made no serious attempt to assimilate Greek scientific culture, or to use the golden opportunities afforded by the cosmopolitan conditions of the age for the transmission of Greek science to the Latin speaking world.

II

BUT while there is no reason to suppose that the Dark Ages were dark because they were religious, it is none the less difficult to exaggerate their darkness, both as regards scientific knowledge, and the completeness of the break between the science of antiquity and the science of modern times. Here the traditional view is justified, and it only becomes false when this judgment is extended from the early to the later Middle Ages so as to make the scientific development of Western

Europe begin with the Renaissance. In reality the recovery of Greek science and the restoration of contact with the main tradition of Greek thought was one of the most striking achievements of mediaeval culture. And it is even more than this: it is a turning point in the history of world civilization, for it marks the passing of the age-long supremacy of Oriental and eastern Mediterranean culture and the beginning of the intellectual leadership of the West. It is in fact a far more important and original achievement than anything that the Renaissance itself accomplished. For the Renaissance scholars, in spite of their originality, were carrying on a tradition that had never been altogether lost: the tradition of humanism and classical scholarship that was founded on Cicero and Quintilian. But the rediscovery of Greek thought by the mediaeval scholars was a new fact in the history of the West: it was the conquest of a new world.

It is true that the scientific renaissance of the Middle Ages was far from being the unaided work of Western thinkers. It was not the result of a gradual process of experiment and discovery, but rather of the importation into Christendom of a scientific tradition and a scientific literature that belonged to an alien culture. Thus it is a parallel phenomenon to the rise of the new lyric poetry and the new literary culture of which I speak in the following chapter. Like the latter it had its origin in the mixed culture of the Western Mediterranean, a world that is strangely neglected by the historian, but which is a key position for the understanding of later mediaeval culture. It was here, in Spain and Sicily, in the trading cities of the French and Italian Rivieras, and at the feudal courts of Provence and Catalonia, that the Christians first met the Arabs and the Jews on equal terms, and came under the influence of the brilliant civilization that had developed in Western Islam from the tenth to the twelfth centuries. It was here that the eyes of Western scholars were first opened to the riches of Greek and Arabic learning and to their own scientific backwardness; and it was here, at Toledo and Salerno and Barcelona and Segovia and Palermo, that the Christians put themselves to school with the Arabs and the Jews and laid the foundations of the new scientific culture of the West.

The cosmopolitan character of the movement is shown by the names of the scholars to whom the introduction of the new knowledge was due. These include Italians like Plato of Tivoli, Gerard of Cremona, and Burgundio and Leonard of Pisa; Sicilian Greeks such as Henry Aristippus and Eugenius the Emir; Spaniards like Gundissalinus, Hugh of Santalla, and Mark of Toledo; Englishmen, such as Adelard of Bath, Robert of Chester, Daniel of Morley and Alfred of Sereshel, a Scot, the famous Michael, a Slav, Hermann of Carinthia, and a Fleming, Rudolf of Bruges.

Apart from the Sicilians and from Burgundio of Pisa, who translated direct from the Greek, all these scholars owed much to the collaboration of men of Arabic speech. Some of them were Mozarabs—Spanish Christians of Arabic speech, like Galippus, the assistant of Gerard of Cremona, but the majority of them were Jews or converts from Judaism, such as John of Seville, (John Abendaud) who worked with Gundissalinus as well as independently, Savasorda, the assistant of Plato of Tivoli, and Petrus Alfonsi, who seems to have visited England in the reign of Henry I.

Nevertheless, the derivative character of the movement and its relative lack of originality ought not to detract from the achievement of these Western scholars who faced so many difficulties and overcame so many obstacles in the disinterested pursuit of scientific knowledge. For, however strange their scientific ideas may seem to us, there can be no doubt that the ideal which inspired their activity was a genuinely scientific one and that they are the humble and half forgotten founders of the long and glorious line of Western scientists.

They were themselves by no means unconscious of the greatness of the issues at stake or of the revolutionary character of their work. One of the early translators, Plato of Tivoli, prefaces his translation of Al Battani's treatise on astronomy[1] with a remarkable indictment of the Western attitude towards science. He attacks the ignorance and sloth that have led the Latins to neglect scientific studies for easier and less worthy pursuits. Rome, he says, has surpassed not only the Greeks but every other people in warlike powers and in the extent of its empire. But with regard to the sciences, Rome has remained inferior by far, not only to the Egyptians and the Greeks, the founders of all the liberal arts, but also to the Arabs.

This holds good of all the arts, for the Latins possess them only in so far as they have received them from others, but it is true above all of astronomy, which

[1] *De Motu Stellarum*, a work of great importance, not only for astronomical science, but because it helped to introduce trigonometry into Western Europe.

surpasses all the other sciences in exactness of method, subtlety of reasoning, and completeness of proof. "In astronomy the Latin world cannot show—I do not say a single author—but even a single translator of whom it can boast. The Egyptians have a multitude of masters in this art, of whom Hermes is the chief; the Greeks have Aristotle, Abrachis (Hipparchus), Ptolemy and innumerable others; the Arabs have Algorithm, (Al Khwarizmi), Messehala, Albategni (Al Battani) and many more. But the Latins on the contrary have not a single author: for books they have only follies, dreams and old wives' fables. This is the reason that has moved me, Plato of Tivoli, to enrich our tongue with that which it lacked the most, by drawing on the treasures of an unknown language."[2]

But if the scholars of the West had a great deal of ground to make up, they lost no time in doing so. The activity of the translators and adapters, above all of Gerard of Cremona, who worked at Toledo until his death in 1187, is almost incredible. In the space of little more than half a century the main tradition of Greek and Arabic learning, both philosophical and scientific, was transmitted to the Latin world—Euclid, Ptolemy, the Arabic mathematicians and astronomers, Galen, Avicenna, Al Farabi, Ibn Gebirol,—but above all Aristotle, whose figure dominates the scientific tradition of both the Greeks and the Arabs, as it was also to dominate that of the mediaeval West.

[2] P. Duhem, *Le Système du Monde de Platon à Copernic*, III, pp. 199-200.

III

THE impact of this great mass of new knowledge on the
Western mind could not but produce startling effects. It
raised the whole question of the relations between religion and science, and between reason and faith, in a very
sharp and accentuated way. The full realization of the
issues at stake was indeed delayed until the strict Aristotelianism of Averroes was introduced into the West
in the first half of the thirteenth century, but they were
already implicit in the scientific doctrines that began
to reach Western Europe a century earlier with Adelard of Bath and Plato of Tivoli.

For the new scientific doctrines were not simply an
addition to the common stock of knowledge which
Western culture already possessed. They formed part
of an organized system of thought which embraced
every aspect of reality. The logical completeness and
consistency of this system made it almost impossible
to accept any part of it without assenting to the whole,
to separate its physical from its metaphysical elements
or to accept its explanation of natural phenomena while
rejecting its theory of spiritual being. And hence, as the
theologians of Islam had long ago realized, Hellenic
science was not the obedient servant of revealed religion, but an independent and rival power. It was a danger alike to Christianity, to Judaism and to Islam, since
it challenged the fundamental dogmas that were common to the three religions; the doctrine of creation,
the docrine of personal immortality, and the belief in

a personal Deity who governed the world by His providence and the free exercise of His omnipotent will.

Science always tends towards determinism, and Aristotelian science was perhaps the most thorough going system of determinism that has ever been invented, since it embraced spirit as well as matter in the working of its mechanism. For this reason, the determinism of the Aristotelians was entirely different to that of modern science. The latter starts from the bottom, with physics and chemistry, and builds up its structure of reality from the atom and the electron. The Aristotelian starts at the top with the movements of the heavenly bodies and finds in them the principle that governs the laws of terrestrial change. Both systems are mechanical, but that of the moderns is a soulless and automatic mechanism, while that of the Greeks is animate and intelligent. In fact, so far from eliminating the idea of God as an unnecessary hypothesis, God is, for Aristotle, the mainspring of his whole system of physics, and the motor that drives the world machine.

Mind is the one principle of movement and order in the world. Without it the universe would be an inert mass, a shapeless chaos. And it is in the eternal and regular movements of the stars that the presence of divine intelligence is most indubitably manifested. They are "the radiant rejoicing, intelligent Sons of Heaven," "visible Gods," in Plato's words, whose ordered march governs the recurrent changes of the time process and the cycles of generation and corruption in the sublunary world.[3]

[3] These views are very fully expounded by Adelard of Bath in his *Questiones Naturales*, c. 74-77: "If reason and foresight exist

All this is very alien to modern ways of thought; for we are accustomed to regard regular movement as characteristic of blind natural forces, and our idea of an intelligent being is that of one which is always doing something different. But to the Greek mind the more regular a movement, the more intelligent must be the mover, and if the stars had not been guided by conscious intelligence, they would stand still or fall blindly through space, like the atoms of Epicurus, without following any regular orbit. In fact one might say that the Greeks would have revered the man who planned the Inner Circle on the Underground Railway as a truly wise and good man, while they would regard the erratic and aimless course of the man who motors for pleasure and speed as evidence of an incurably weak and vicious mind.

Now the mediaeval mind was certainly nearer to

even in our dark and perturbed lower world, how much more must the stars employ intelligence in their determined and constant courses." "The man who contends that the stars are senseless must himself be without sense." (Thorndyke, *Magic and Experimental Science*, II, 40-1.) St Thomas himself states that no wise man doubts that all natural motions of inferior bodies are caused by the motions of the celestial bodies since it is proved both by reason and experience. (*Responsio ad J. de Vercellis*, cited Thorndyke, *op. cit.*, II, 609 from *Opera* (Paris ed.), vol. 27, p. 249.) So too Albertus Magnus admits that the whole world of terrestrial nature is governed by the movements of the stars. He tends, however, to minimize the importance of the celestial intelligences and concentrates the emphasis of his theory on the First Mover. *Sicut manus est instrumentum intellectus practici in artificialibus, ita totus caelestis circulus est instrumentum hujus intellectus ad totum materiam naturae quae ambit. Metaphysicorum* XI, ii, 12. Thorndyke, II, 581.

that of the Greeks than is our own. But for all that they were on our side of the gulf that divides the ancient from the modern world. Spirit and matter no longer formed part of a single indivisible unity. God was not an abstract intelligence that acted as the magneto of the cosmic dynamo, but the Heavenly Father, the Creator and Saviour of Mankind. The cosmic process was no eternal cycle, but a spiritual drama with a beginning and an end, and the earth, instead of being the passive recipient of the planetary influences, the slave of fate and necessity, was a battleground on which supreme spiritual issues were decided.

To men who had been reared in this spiritual tradition the theories of Graeco-Arabic science came as intruders from an alien world. They regarded them with the instinctive distrust and aversion with which the orthodox circles received the new geological and biological theories in the last century. William of Auvergne, the most representative figure among the schoolmen of the older tradition in the first half of the thirteenth century, sums up the orthodox view in the following sentences: "As for the Christian people, wholly dedicated to virtue and holiness and the service of the Creator, it has been occupied very little with Philosophy, save when the perversity of heretics and the objections of fools have compelled it to defend its religion and its faith and to destroy the doctrines that are opposed to its salvation and contrary to the honour of God. The men of this religion have been concerned with their souls and have not troubled themselves about the souls of the heavens. It has seemed to them that, from the point of view of their religion and their eternal salvation, there was neither profit to be gained from knowing about these souls nor loss from ignoring them. Whether the world may be a single animate body or not, whether the entire heaven should be an animate being or the different heavens animate beings—these are questions that the Christian people has regarded with horror and treated as monstrous. It is plunged in astonishment by this discussion which has hitherto been entirely unknown to it, and in which it sees a novelty that does not concern it at all."[4]

But if orthodox thinkers like William of Auvergne could look with indifference on the cosmological theories of the neo-Aristotelians, it was a very different thing when the latter came to apply those theories to the world of men. For the Arabs, following the traditions of later Greek thought, taught that mankind no less than the celestial spheres derived its activity from a spiritual principle—the active intelligence. In other words Reason was not a faculty of the human soul, but a cosmic principle—the lowest in the hierarchy of spiritual substances—and man attained to rational activity only in so far as his passive and mortal intelligence became temporarily actuated by this immortal and impersonal power. This doctrine struck at the very heart of religious faith, since it involved the denial of personal immortality, and consequently William of Auvergne declared that it was no subject for philosophical discussion, but a deadly heresy which should be rooted out "with fire and sword and every kind of torture." It was, in fact, to remain a burning question for three hundred years and more, but even before it

[4] William of Paris, *Opera* (1516), *tom.* II, cap. VII, 195, quoted in Duhem, *op. cit.*, IV, 318.

had become a living issue, the authorities had already realised the danger to religious orthodoxy implicit in Aristotelian science, and a series of episcopal and papal pronouncements, from 1210 onwards, were directed against the study of the physics and metaphysics of Aristotle at the University of Paris which had now become the acknowledged centre of Western thought.

Nevertheless ecclesiastical authority and theological traditionalism were alike powerless to check the advance of the new knowledge. In spite of the protests of conservative thinkers such as William of Auvergne and St Bonaventure, in spite of successive attempts to forbid the study and teaching of Aristotelian science in the University of Paris, the new ideas proved irresistibly attractive and even the extreme conclusions of Averroistic rationalism found a hearing. There was a real danger that religion and science would declare war on one another and that Western thought would be sacrificed, like that of Islam, to the conflict between the orthodox fideism of the theologians and the scientific rationalism of the Aristotelians. Fortunately for Western culture, however, the issues were never narrowed to this dilemma. The vitality of mediaeval religion shows itself in the eagerness and intellectual courage with which the leaders of Christian thought such as Grosseteste, Albert the Great, Thomas of York, Thomas Aquinas and Roger Bacon confronted the new situation and strove to assimilate the new knowledge. It is true that traditionalists like St Bonaventure and Bishop Tempier attempted to resist the new movement of thought and to involve the Christian Aristotelianism of St Thomas in the same condemnation as that of the Averroists. In 1277 Bishop Tempier, supported by John Peckham, the disciple of St Bonaventure and the future Archbishop of Canterbury, issued a sweeping condemnation of modern errors which was aimed impartially at the three leading representatives of the new movement of thought: Siger of Brabant, Roger Bacon, and Thomas Aquinas. The result of this decree was the imprisonment of Siger and Roger Bacon, and the exclusion of Thomism from the schools of Paris and Oxford. Nevertheless this was only a local and temporary reaction. The condemnation of Thomism was not confirmed by the Papacy, which recognized the importance of the new learning and which finally set the seal of its approval on St Thomas's ideal of a reconciliation between Aristotelian science and the Christian Faith.

IV

THE inaugurator of this work of reconciliation was the German, Albertus Magnus, the most learned man of the thirteenth century, and the most complete embodiment of the different intellectual currents of his age. He is the master, on the one hand, of St Thomas and the Christian Aristotelians, and, on the other, of Ulrich of Strasburg and the Christian Neo-Platonists. His greatest achievement was to put the whole *corpus* of Graeco-Arabic thought at the disposal of Western scholasticism through the encyclopaedic series of commentaries and expositions by which, as he said, he made "all the parts of philosophy, physics, metaphysics and mathematics, intelligible to the Latins." Nor was he merely a passive intermediary between two intellectual traditions, like the translators of the previous century; he had a really original mind, and his scientific observations, above all in biology, botany and geology, were among the first independent achievements of Western European science. It is indeed in science rather than in philosophy that his originality is to be found. As a philosopher he tended rather to syncretism than to synthesis, and his philosophical works form a kind of metaphysical museum in which theories of very diverse origin find themselves side by side.

The true creator of the Aristotelian-Christian synthesis was not the German encyclopaedist but his Neapolitan pupil, St Thomas, through whom the mind of Western Christendom finally succeeded in completely incorporating the intellectual heritage of the Aristotelian tradition. Nature had fitted him for his task. He was no child of the Gothic North, like Albert or Abelard, but a native of that strange borderland of Western civilization where feudal Europe mingled with the Greek and Saracen worlds. He sprang from a family of courtiers and troubadours whose fortunes were intimately bound up with the brilliant half-oriental, half-humanist court of the great Hohenstaufen emperor and his ill-fated successors—that court which was at once the cradle of Italian literature and one of the main channels through which Arabic science reached the Christian world. St Thomas was born at the time when Michael Scot, under the patronage of the emperor, was making the first Latin translations of the great Aristotelian commentaries of Averroes. He was educated at the University of Naples, the first university to owe its foundation and organization to the state, and he received his philosophical initiation from Peter of Ireland, one of the first Western scholastics who came under the influence of Averroistic thought. Nevertheless, St Thomas was never a pupil of the Arabs in the same sense as the majority of his contemporaries. With him the Western mind emancipates itself from its Arabic teachers and returns to the sources. Indeed, there is in St Thomas a real intellectual affinity to the Greek genius. More than any other Western thinker, mediaeval or modern, he possessed the tranquil lucidity and the gift of abstract intelligence that mark the Hellenic mind.

Thus he was peculiarly fitted to interpret the thought of Aristotle to his age without either forcing it into the mould of an alien mentality or disregarding the autonomy and transcendence of the Christian faith. Unlike the many mediaeval thinkers, both Christian and oriental, who evolved a kind of theosophical syncretism that was irreconcileable alike with the ideal of religious faith and with that of a purely rational philosophy, St Thomas was able to combine the peripatetic tradition in philosophy and the patristic tradition in theology without falsifying either of them. It is true that his thought was Neoplatonic rather than Aristotelian in its concentration on spiritual reality and its consecration to a religious ideal. Nevertheless, although the mind of St Thomas was steeped in the thought of St Augustine and the Pseudo-Dionysius, his philosophy marks a complete break with the old Augustinian Neoplatonic idealism that had hitherto dominated the intellectual development of the West. Not only did St Thomas accept the cardinal principles of Aristotelian physics, but he applied them resolutely to the nature of man, teaching that matter is the principle of human individuation, and that the soul is the form of the body. Hence man is not, as the Platonists believed, a spiritual being temporarily confined in the prison of the flesh, a stranger in an alien world, he is a part of nature—that dynamic order which embraces the whole series of living beings from man to plant, as well as the things that are without life but not without their principle of form. And so the human intelligence is not that of a pure spirit which exists only for the contemplation of absolute reality. It is consubstantial with matter, sub-ject to the conditions of space and time and it can only construct an intelligible order out of the data of sens-ible experience, systematized by the scientific activity of reason. Thus while on the one hand human reason is distinctively animal, the lowest and most obscured form of intelligence, on the other hand, it is the one principle of spiritual order in nature, and it is its essent-ial function to reduce the unintelligible chaos of the material world to reason and order.

This theory of the human intelligence is the essential doctrine of Thomism and the keystone of the Christian Aristotelian synthesis. Hitherto both the Averroist and the Christian Platonist had regarded the spiritual prin-ciple of intelligence as something superhuman and divine. It was not *in* man as a part of his personality; it was a power which illuminated his mind from outside, whether it be regarded with the Christian Platonists as the ray of Divine Light that illuminates the immortal human soul, or whether, as Averroes taught, it was the power of a universal intelligence actuating the successive, transitory and mortal minds of men. To St Thomas, on the other hand, the active intelligence is the very essence of the soul and the root of human responsibility and liberty. "For if," he writes, "the active intellect is a substance outside man, the whole of man's activity depends on an extrinsic principle. Man then will not be a free agent but will be acted upon by another, and so he will not be the master of his own acts nor deserve praise or blame; and the whole of moral science and social intercourse will perish—*quod est inconveniens.*"[5]

This insistence on the rationality and freedom of the individual personality is a new note in mediaeval thought. It marks the end of the oriental and Byzantine absorption of the human mind in the Absolute and the Transcendent, and the beginning of the distinctively Western ideal of a philosophy of man and of the human mind: a philosophy which recognizes the dependence of human knowledge on sensible experience without excluding it from the world of spiritual reality and religious truth. The intellectualism of St Thomas is equally remote from an absolute idealism and a rationalist empiricism, from the metaphysical mysticism of the ancient East and from the scientific materialism of the modern West. It recognized the autonomous rights of the human reason and its scientific activity against the absolutism of a purely theological ideal of knowledge, and the rights of human nature and natural morality against the exclusive domination of the ascetic ideal, while in social life it substituted for the all-em-

[5] *Summa Contra Gentiles,* II, c. 76 *ad fin.*

bracing unity of the Byzantine and Islamic theocracy
the dual order of Church and State, each with its independent functions and its own principle of authority. Thus, though Thomism did far less for humane
letters than the school of Chartres in the preceding
century, it opened the way for humanism in the larger
sense of the word, and though its scientific achievements were very inferior to those of the fourteenth-
century Nominalists, it opened the way for an autonomous and disinterested scientific activity.

The comparative sterility of Thomism in natural
science has a twofold cause. On the one hand it is due
to its concentration on metaphysics and theology, and
on the other to the very completeness of its synthesis
with the Aristotelian tradition. The Aristotelian *corpus*
supplied the Middle Ages with an organized body of
scientific knowledge far in advance of anything that
Western culture had hitherto known, and consequently it was accepted as the last word in human wisdom.

In this respect Aristotelian scholasticism tended towards the standpoint of Averroes, who regards Aristotle as the divinely appointed hierophant of the mysteries of nature. "It is he," wrote Averroes, "who has
discovered the three sciences—Physics, Logic and
Metaphysics, and who has completed them. He has
discovered them, for what we find of this knowledge
in the writings of the earlier authors is not worthy of
being considered even as a part of this doctrine, and
one can say without hesitation that it does not even
contain the principles of it. He has completed them,
for none of those that have come after him, even to the
present day, has added anything to them; nor has any-

one discovered in his words an error of any importance."

"Let us praise God who in the domain of perfection
has singled out this man from all others and has conferred on him in particular the dignity of humanity
carried to its culminating point in such a measure as no
other man in any age has been able to reach."[6]

V

THIS attitude to Aristotle is often regarded as typical
of the authoritarianism and dogmatism of mediaeval
Christian scholasticism. Actually, however, it has nothing to do with religion and is even more characteristic of the Aristotelian rationalism of the Averroists
than of the Christian Aristotelianism of the Thomists.
The influence of St Thomas on modern Catholic
thought is apt to make us exaggerate the completeness
of his victory, so that he appears to us the philosophical
dictator of the mediaeval world. We forget the immense prestige of Averroism, which maintained the
tradition of a non-Christian Aristotelianism right
through the later Middle Ages, and which, even in the
later Renaissance, was still the most formidable oppon-
ent of the new European science. In fact, the rationalist
orthodoxy of the Averroists proved a greater obstacle
to scientific progress than the obscurantism of conserv-

[6] From the preface to the Great Commentary of Aristotle *De
physico auditu* and from the paraphrase to the *De generatione ani-
malium*, lib. I, cap. 20, quoted by Mandonnet, *Siger de Brabant*,
1st ed., p. 153 and by Duhem, *op. cit.*, IV, pp. 310-11.

ative theologians. If the new scientific and philosophical culture of the West had been purely Aristotelian, it would probably have been no less sterile than the scientific culture of Islam in the later Middle Ages. But mediaeval Aristotelianism never possessed a monopoly in Western thought, it was counter-balanced by the existence of another intellectual tradition—that of Christian Platonism—which contributed no less to the new scientific development, and which is equally characteristic of mediaeval culture. This tradition was no more independent of oriental influences than was that of Albertus Magnus and St Thomas. It also incorporated considerable Aristotelian elements, just as Thomism preserved a large element of Platonism.

But while the Aristotelian element in the Thomist synthesis represents a relatively pure peripatetic tradition, the Aristotelianism of the Platonists was derived from the school of Al Farabi and Avicenna, and was already heavily charged with Neoplatonic elements: in other words, it was the synthesis of a synthesis.

The mediaeval Platonists, like their predecessors, differed from the disciples of Aristotle above all in their theory of knowledge. Sensible experience only gives a knowledge of sensible things, but the higher knowledge springs from the illumination of the mind by divine truth: it is intuitive and spiritual. Hence the true source of knowledge is not to be found in things, but in the divine ideas, the *rationes aeternae*, that are the ultimate foundation of reality. And this theory of knowledge naturally leads to the Platonic, as opposed to the Aristotelian theory of science. Though the Augustinians did not go so far as Plato and deny that

any science of sensible things was possible, they did
tend to exalt the deductive over the inductive method,
to regard mathematics as the model science and to pre-
fer the sciences that make use of mathematical methods,
such as optics and astronomy, to the non-mathema-
tical Aristotelian sciences of physics and biology. The
most remarkable representative of this tendency was
Robert Grosseteste, one of the most original and many-
sided minds of the thirteenth century.[7] Influenced on
the one hand by the Neoplatonic and Augustinian
conception of Light as a type of spiritual reality and, on
the other, by the Arabic works on optics and perspective of the great eleventh-century physicist Ibn al
Haitham (Alhazen), he attempted to deduce from the
nature of light a complete cosmological theory. Light
is not only the primary substance, it is the very cause of
the extension of matter. It alone is auto-diffusive, for
given a luminous point, it at once creates for itself a
sphere of illumination. Thus it is the infinite dynamic
energy of light that generates the finite *quantum* and
confers on matter its form and dimensions.[8]

This view of space as essentially the field of radiation
of energy is curiously suggestive of modern physical
theory, and no less modern is the scientific ideal of the
mathematical explanation of nature which is associated
with it in Grosseteste's philosophy. Since the laws of
perspective—of optical geometry—are the foundation

[7] It is a remarkable fact that the only thirteenth-century philosophers who read Aristotle in the original and translated his
works directly from the Greek were the two leading Platonists
of the age—Robert Grosseteste and William of Moerbeke.

[8] Baur, *Die Philosophie des Robert Grosseteste*, (1917) 76-84.

of physical reality, mathematics are the only path to the understanding of nature. "All causes of natural effects," he writes, "can be given by lines and angles and figures, without them it is impossible to understand natural philosophy. For they hold good in the whole universe and in its parts absolutely."[9]

These ideas are like the inspired guesses of the early Greek physicists. They were too far in advance of the contemporary state of science to bear immediate fruit, and it was not until the age of Galileo and Descartes that they were actually realizable. Nevertheless, the influence of Grosseteste on the thought of his age was far from being negligible. His scientific ideas, above all his faith in mathematical reasoning, influenced the direction of studies at the new University of Oxford which he did so much to organize and in the Franciscan Order of which he was the patron. Throughout the thirteenth century and the first half of the fourteenth, Oxford maintained the tradition of Augustinian philosophy and of 'mathematical' science, and it was from Oxford that the remarkable development of scientific thought in France during the fourteenth century derived its inspiration.

Moreover, it is difficult to overestimate the influence of Grosseteste's thought on the mind of one of the most remarkable figures of the thirteenth century, whose fame has indeed overshadowed that of his master—I mean Roger Bacon. It was from Grosseteste that Bacon derived not only his distinctive philosophical and scientific views, above all his conviction of the importance of mathematics, but also his interest in philology

[9] Baur, *op. cit.*, 92-93.

and in the study of Greek and the oriental languages, of which Grosseteste was one of the pioneers. But if Bacon owed far more to his predecessors than has usually been supposed, he was none the less a profoundly original mind. His originality is however to be found less in his scientific theories than in his personality, and in his general attitude to contemporary thought. To a far greater extent than Grosseteste he stands apart from the main current of scholastic philosophical study, he belongs rather to the tradition of the men of science who were responsible for the introduction of Arabic science into the West, such as Adelard of Bath, Gerard of Cremona and Plato of Tivoli. It is true that he speaks with contempt of the translators, but this is owing to a somewhat exaggerated sense of their linguistic incompetence and not from any doubt as to the value of Arabic science, which he regards as the main channel by which Christendom could recover the wisdom of the ancient world. He resembles Adelard above all in his critical attitude to Western scholasticism; indeed, he quotes the actual words of Adelard with regard to the danger of a blind reliance on authority. In Bacon's view, the four fundamental obstacles to the progress of philosophy are dependence on authority, the influence of custom, the ignorance of the populace and the false pretensions of those who esteem themselves to be learned. He cannot find words strong enough to express his contempt for "these new theologians" of the teaching orders who become masters in theology and philosophy before they have studied, and who console themselves for their ignorance by belittling the sciences

and display their emptiness before the eyes of the ignorant multitude.

Yet although Bacon includes the great Dominicans,
Albert and Thomas, in his wholesale condemnation,
he is far far from hostile to the new learning. He dismiss-
es Alexander of Hales, precisely because the latter had
had no training in Aristotelian physics and metaphysics
"which are the glory of our modern studies." The
works of Aristotle are for him "the foundation of all
wisdom," and he blames his contemporaries not for
their cultivation of Aristotelian science, but for their
misunderstanding and corruption of it.

Still less can we regard his attitude to scholasticism
and authority as an attempt to free science and reason
from their dependence on theology. In this respect he
is distinctly reactionary in comparison with St Thomas.
The unity of science in which he believes is a purely
theological unity. To an even greater extent than the
earlier Augustinians he is prepared to subordinate all
human knowledge to the divine wisdom that is contained in the Scriptures. All knowledge springs ultimately from Revelation. The first and most perfect
scientists were the patriarchs, and the philosophers of
the Gentiles merely collected the crumbs that had fall-
en from the tables of Shem and Abraham and Solomon.
He admits the possibility of scientific progress, for
there is no finality in this life, and knowledge must con-
tinue to increase with the rise and fall of the world religions.[10] All the signs, he believed, pointed to the ap-

[10] Thus the conjunction of Jupiter with Mars marks the rise of
the religion of the Chaldeans, with the sun that of the Egyptians,

proaching end of the age and to the coming of Antichrist, and it was to arm Christendom for the struggle
and to prepare the way for its renovation under the
leadership of a great Pope and a great king that he pro-
pounded his schemes for the reform of studies and the
utilization of the power of science.

Thus Bacon was no devotee of knowledge for its
own sake. His attitude is fundamentally far less rational
and far less intellectualist than that of Aristotle or even
that of St Thomas. But though this detracts from the
philosophic value of his work, it does nothing to dimin-
ish his personal originality and his historical significance.
For the greatness of Roger Bacon consists not in his
scientific achievement, which was small, nor in his
scientific method, which was inferior to that of his
master, Peter of Maricourt, the obscure *Magister Ex-
perimentorum*. His greatness is to be found in the
scientific vision and imagination which made him the
discoverer of a new scientific ideal and the prophet of
the new world of modern science.

For the history of science is not that of a simple continuous development. It takes a different form in every culture, Babylonian, Greek, Moslem and Christian, and
until a culture has created a scientific ideal that is in harmony with its own spirit, it cannot bear scientic fruit.
In the thirteenth century Western Christendom had
already acquired a considerable knowledge of both
Greek and Arabic science, but it knew them as it were

with Venus that of the Saracens, with Mercury that of the Christians, and finally the conjunction of Jupiter with the Moon
marks the coming of Antichrist. *De Viciis Contractis in Studio
Theologie*, ed. Steele, pp. 43-50.

from outside, since neither the Greek nor the Arabic ideal of science answered to the needs of Western culture or could be fully assimilated by the Western mind.

The Greek ideal of science was essentially intellectualist. It was the contemplation of reality as an intelligible order. To the Greek mind the practical results of science were quite a secondary matter; indeed, in their eyes the application of science to mechanical ends seemed rather vulgar and childish. The end of science was not to do but to know: *felix qui potuit rerum cognocere causas.* The reward of the scientist was to share the blessedness of the immortal gods who are eternally satisfied with the contemplation of the ordered course of the heavens and the vision of eternal law.

Now, this attitude of mind was as incomprehensible to the mediaeval Christian as it is to the modern Englishman. William of Auvergne, whom I have already quoted on the subject, treats the Hellenic cosmology with the rude common sense of a Philistine and irreverently compares the intelligences that move the heavenly spheres to a donkey turning a treadmill, the only difference, he says, being that the movement of the donkey serves some purpose, whereas the gyrations of the heavenly intelligences do no good to anybody. It is true that St Thomas does not talk in this way. He at least could understand something of the Greek point of view, for he was an intellectualist himself and believed that man's highest good was to understand. Nevertheless, as a Christian he believed that this Good was to be found in the knowledge of God and spiritual things rather than in the science of nature. Moreover his very intellectualism led him to despise the flux of material being—"those lower things which are subject to generation and corruption and are the least part of the universe and the furthest removed from intelligible order."[11] Hence the Hellenism of St Thomas finds expression not in physical science but in his religious and metaphysical thought. He is the scientist of the spiritual world.

But it was only a few rare minds in the Middle Ages —men such as St Thomas and Grosseteste and Albert the Great—which attained any real contact with the Hellenic tradition. The living tradition of science was that of the Arabs, and the science of the Arabs was entirely different in its inner form and spirit to the science of the Greeks. No doubt the Arabic scientists were the heirs of the Greek tradition and were not unworthy of their inheritance. But while they preserved it they unconsciously transformed it by infusing a different spirit into it. In spite of its achievements Arabic science belongs to the same world as the Arabian Nights—a world of magic and mystery—and the scientist was the man who could control these mysterious forces by the power of secret knowledge. What he sought was not knowledge, but Power, to discover the Elixir of Life, the Philosopher's Stone, the Talisman, the Word of Power, and the magic properties of plants and minerals. His astronomy was inseparable from astrology, and his chemistry from alchemy. In a word, Arabic science was magic.

Now when the tide of Arabic learning reached the West, it brought with it this conception of science.

[11] *De Spiritualibus Creaturis*, 8.

The first translators and men of science, such as Adelard of Bath, Plato of Tivoli and Roger of Hereford, were primarily interested in astrology, and it is easy to understand how popular opinion came to regard men like Michael Scot and Roger Bacon as wizards and magicians. And Roger Bacon himself seems at first sight to belong entirely to the Arabic scientific tradition. Like the Arabs he believed that science was power and that the scientist was a wonder worker and a magician; and the very titles of his books on alchemy,[12] for example, *Of the Marvellous Power of Art and Nature, an epistle of the secret works of Nature, Liber secretorum de spiritu occulto* and *The Book of the Green Lion*,—are typical of the esoteric attitude to science which I have spoken of as characteristically oriental. Even his theory of experimental science, which has been regarded as an anticipation of modern scientific method, is by no means free from this magical element. For Bacon's experimental science is not the verification of hypothesis by experiment: it is not the inductive method that had already been so admirably described by Aristotle in the Posterior Analytics; it is essentially an esoteric science, the knowledge that teaches man to transmute metals, to read the future in the stars and to prolong human life for centuries.

All this is true; yet none the less Bacon is profoundly original and a genuine precursor and prophet of Western science. In spite of its fantastic claims, his experimental science is not magic but *applied science*, and his scientist is not a magician but an expert. For Bacon realized both the limitless possibilities of scientific

[12] Some of them, however, are probably not authentic.

knowledge, and also its potential dangers, and his desire to confine experimental science to a class of chosen
initiates was due not to occultism, but to his fear of the
new knowledge being perverted to anti-social ends.
His scientific ideal was essentially a utilitarian one.
Science existed not for its own sake, not for private
ends, but for the service of divine wisdom and "the
guidance of the whole world." His ideal was no less
theocratic than that of his contemporaries, but whereas
they conceived this ideal primarily as the subordina-
tion of the temporal to the spiritual power, Bacon believed that it could only be realized by the coopera-
tion of science. As philosophy was the handmaid of
theology, so experimental science was the handmaid
of philosophy, and it was the divinely ordained instrument by which the Church could fulfil its mission towards mankind and bring about the kingdom of God
on earth. If the Church made use of this instrument she
could rule the whole world and subdue the infidel, as
she failed to do by the bloody and wasteful method of
the Crusades. Experimental science was inevitably an
esoteric tradition confined to a small body of experts.
If these experts were left to their own devices, they
might become an anti-social force, as was the case
with the magicians and the astrologers. It was, therefore, necessary that the Papacy should take control and
organize a select body of scientists which would be, as
it were, the brain of Christendom.

This grandiose vision of a world ruled by a science
dedicated to moral and spiritual ends, has an importance
that far transcends the half scientific, half magical forms
in which Bacon embodied it, since it marks the emer-

gence of the new ideal that was to dominate the development of Western science. For after all it is not the intellectualist ideal of pure science—the 'theory' of an
intelligible order—but Bacon's ideal of science as an
instrument of world conquest, a means for the subjection of nature to the service of man, which is that of
the modern world. The former looks backward to the
classical perfection of the Hellenic world, the latter
looks forward to the brilliant and disorderly progress
of the Western mind. When Bacon sings the praises of
the experimental science that can create automobiles
and flying machines and devices that will destroy a
whole army at once, he is the prophet of modern
science, nor can we, in these days of mechanized warfare and mechanized production, afford altogether to
despise his warnings of the danger of allowing these
vast forces to escape moral direction and social control.

No doubt there is an immense gap between Bacon's
prophetic vision and its realization by modern science.
Nevertheless it was not merely a fruit of the imagination of a pseudo-scientific charlatan. The seeds of the
new Western scientific development were already being sown in the thirteenth century. At the very time
when Roger Bacon was dreaming dreams and seeing
visions of the future of experimental science, his master,
Peter of Maricourt, was already giving a striking example of the genuine experimental method in his
treatise on the Magnet, which was composed, signifi-
cantly enough, in the camp of the crusading army before the Saracen city of Lucera in Apulia in 1269. For in
spite of the imposing appearance of Arabic science, the
intellectual leadership was already passing to the youn-

ger culture of Western Christendom. Western mathematics were being reborn with Leonard of Pisa and Jordan Nemorarius and Grosseteste, and there were already signs of the advent of the new science of mechanics which is, as it were, the scientific expression of the dynamic spirit of Western culture and through which Bacon's vision of the application of mathematics to practical ends was one day to be realized.

Moreover, Bacon's own teaching was not so lacking in influence as has usually been supposed. As Duhem has shown, the leading writers on astronomy in the next generation—Bernard of Verdun, William of St Cloud, and John of Sicily, not to mention Peter d'Ailly at a later date—were among his followers. And apart from this direct or semi-direct influence, the spirit of his teaching, with its appeal from authority to experience and its exaltation of mathematical reasoning, survives in the tradition of critical and scientific Nominalism which was the dominant force in the intellectual life of the fourteenth century. In the schoolmen of that age—William Ockam, John Buridan, Albert of Saxony and Nicholas Oresme—we find not only a critical reaction against the authority of Aristotelian and Arabic tradition, but also an original movement of scientific research which prepares the way for the coming of Leonardo da Vinci and Copernicus and the science of the Renaissance.

Thus the strictly theological tradition of mediaeval thought —the tradition of St Augustine and St Bernard, which finds its complete thirteenth-century representative in St Bonaventure—is not the only intellectual element in mediaeval culture. The latter widens out in the thirteenth century to include, on the one hand, the philosophic humanism of St Thomas which represents the birth of Western philosophy and, on the other, the scientific idealism of Roger Bacon which marks the emergence, if not of Western science, at least of a new scientific ideal. No doubt, in this as in so many other respects, the later Middle Ages failed to realize the brilliant promise of their earlier development. The wide metaphysical vision of the thirteenth century degenerated into the sterile logomachy of the later Scotists, which Sir Thomas More compared to the process of milking a he-goat into a sieve, while the spirit of scientific research which had been so active at Oxford in the thirteenth century and at Paris in the fourteenth, gave place to a blind reliance on authority and an arrogant disregard of new knowledge.

These tendencies in later scholasticism brought it into conflict with the living thought of the age and tended to throw discredit on the whole tradition of mediaeval thought. It was responsible for the belief that scholasticism was essentially anti-scientific and anti-humanist, and that the Middle Ages were a long period of mental degeneration—the night of the human spirit. It is easy to find excuses for the men who originated this view—for the Renaissance men of science and Francis Bacon and the Cartesians—for they were actually suffering under the incubus of an unintelligent traditionalism. But for all that it is a profoundly unhistorical attitude and one that is no less false than that of the Humanist who thought that all the literary and artistic production of the Middle Ages could be dismissed as Gothic barbarism, or as that of the Re-

formers who believed that mediaeval religion was nothing but superstition and apostasy.

RELIGION AND MEDIAEVAL CULTURE

IV
RELIGION & MEDIAEVAL LITERATURE

I

WE have seen how the mediaeval development consisted, above all, in a gradual process of interpenetration between the barbaric
society of the young peoples of Western Europe and
the Christian culture of the later Roman Empire embodied in the Catholic Church. The new peoples received Christianity and in doing so they acquired a
new culture and a new soul.

And nowhere do we see this process so clearly as in
the history of mediaeval literature, for here we are not
forced to rely, as in social history, on partial and fragmentary evidence which at best only throws light on
the surface of the social process; we have the living wit-
ness of the mind of the age that we are studying. It is
true that this evidence also is by no means complete;
there are whole classes and societies that never attained
to literary expression, and while in the early part of the
Middle Ages, at least, much that must once have existed has perished, nevertheless enough remains of
mediaeval literature to make us realize the complexity
of the mediaeval development and the multiplicity of
intellectual strands that have been woven into the pattern of mediaeval culture.

For, as I pointed out in the first chapter, the Christian culture of the later Roman Empire was by no
means a simple and uniform phenomenon. It represents itself a synthesis between two different traditions:
that of the classical culture, and that of Christianity, a
synthesis which was achieved only with difficulty and
on the very eve of the dissolution of the Empire. The
great representatives of Latin-Christian culture—
Ambrose, Jerome, Augustine, Rufinus, Marius Victor-

inus, Prudentius—all flourished in the last days of the
Western Empire and their work was only partially
accomplished when the storm broke. Yet, incomplete
as it was, it was strong enough not only to survive the
downfall of the Empire and of classical civilization,
but to impose itself on the conquering peoples and
become the intellectual patrimony of the new world.
What has perished, strange to say, has not been the
literature of the conquered, but that of the conquerors.
Nothing remains of the old heroic poetry of the Germans in which Charlemagne himself delighted, save a
single fragment. Only in the outer lands, in the British
Isles and in Iceland, did the tradition of vernacular
literature survive unbroken. And consequently the
literature of the Dark Ages is not, as we might expect
it to be, the literature of warlike barbarians; it is a
literature of schoolmasters and grammarians, of com-
mentators and homilists. The children of the barbarians put themselves to school with the monks and the
Fathers, with the result that they wrote the same language and thought the same thoughts. No one could
guess from the study of his works that a man like Bede,
for example, was hardly two generations removed
from pagan barbarism. He belongs rather to the world
of Jerome and Rufinus, and wrote better Latin than
many an educated Roman of the later Empire.

But while the Dark Ages are by no means lacking in
learning or literature, there is no literature that is less
read, or it must be admitted less readable. Of the hundred volumes or so into which Migne has compressed
the literary remains of the period, there are but three or
four which still retain any literary vitality or human

interest. Boethius, Bede, Adamnan, Einhard, Gregory the Great and Gregory of Tours, these, I think, are the only authors that are ever read for their own sake, together with the authors of a few hymns, above all the two famous ones ascribed to Venantius Fortunatus, the *Vexilla Regis* and the *Pange lingua* which give their author the right to the title of the first mediaeval poet. For the rest it is a literature of schoolmasters whose very quotations are not original, but have been borrowed from the writings of some grammarian or epitomist of the later Empire.

It is characteristic of the age that the most famous and popular work that it produced should have been the *Etymologies* of Isidore of Seville—that extraordinary collection of miscellaneous information which was the encyclopaedia of the Dark Ages. Isidore was no doubt the most learned man of his age and thus deserved the praises lavished on him by his contemporaries. But he was by no means as learned as he seems at first sight. All those quotations from Pacuvius, and Afranius and Ennius and Livius Andronicus, which suggest to the unwary reader that Isidore was deeply read in the works of early Roman poets and dramatists that we no longer possess, are in reality lifted bodily and without acknowledgement from the pages of Servius and Festus.

This lack of originality is the most striking feature of later Latin literature, above all in its secular forms. It has nothing to do with the 'monkish obscurantism' of eighteenth-century legend, it was due to the exhaustion of the classical tradition itself—the dying literature of a dying society. Secular literature perished not from

neglect so much as from pedantry. It finds an inglor-
ious end in the morass of sham erudition in which that
amazing pedant Virgilius Maro of Toulouse disports
himself like a hippopotamus at play. It is only in the
religious literature of the time that we find the seeds of
life. The great Passion hymns of Fortunatus stand in an
entirely different category from his secular poetry,
though he himself probably would have rated the
latter far higher. Consequently we have no right to
blame Gregory the Great for his depreciation of secular
culture and his refusal to allow the word of God to be
fettered by the rules of the grammarians, for in this he
is the champion of the rights of the new world, and
he stands for the living culture of the Church and the
religion of the people against the traditionalism of the
rhetoricians and the dead world of classical culture.

But though the Church insisted on the primacy and
the independence of the Christian tradition, she was by
no means unwilling to accept the classical tradition as
an instrument of Christian education and as the vehicle
of Catholic culture. And it was, in fact, this adoption of
the classical tradition by the Church which saved it
from the sterility and emptiness that had destroyed its
secular vitality, and which gave it a new spiritual purpose and a new social function that ensured its survival
and its transmission to the new peoples. If the culture of
the Dark Ages is a culture of schoolmasters, they were
the schoolmasters of Europe, and all the subsequent
achievement of Western culture rests on the foundation
of their work. Hence the real interest of the period lies
not so much in the literature that it produced as in the
educational work that it accomplished by the trans-

mission of classical and patristic literature to the new peoples and the consequent modification of their own cultures.

II

THE most striking example of this process is to be found in Ireland and England, for here it was entirely religious in origin, being wholly due to the work of the monastic schools and missions, owing little or nothing to the social inheritance of the Roman tradition which was so important in Gaul and Italy and Spain. On the continent the Church was Latin not only in its intellectual culture but by its social traditions and its political associations. It remained in a sense the Church of the Empire, even when the Empire had fallen. But in the British Isles it was not so; above all in Ireland, which had no traditional connection with the Roman Empire and which possessed an exceptionally strong and developed form of native culture. Consequently in Ireland alone the native culture met the Latin tradition of the Church on relatively equal terms and it was there that a synthesis of the two elements was achieved which resulted in the formation of a vernacular Christian literature and culture. Nor was the influence of this vernacular culture limited to the Celtic speaking peoples; it was transmitted to Northumbria through the Irish missionaries and was the source and model of the brilliant development of vernacular Anglian culture in the seventh and eighth centuries which created Anglo-Saxon literature. And the Anglo-Saxons in

turn transmitted it to Germany, where the earliest beginnings of vernacular literature are associated with
the missionary activities of Boniface and his Anglo-
Saxon foundations, above all at Fulda, and later with
the old Celtic foundation of St Gall which retained its
contacts with Irish scholarship and culture down to the
eleventh century.

It is a characteristic feature of this culture that though
it was essentially monastic, its interests were not confined to ecclesiastical literature. We owe to it the preservation of the heroic epic traditions, not only in Ireland,
but also in England, with Beowulf and Waldere, and
in Germany, where it was a monk of Fulda who saved
for us the only remaining relic of the old German heroic
poetry, the *Hildebrandslied*.

It is difficult to exaggerate the importance of this
'insular' Celtic-Anglo-Saxon tradition of vernacular
culture in the history of the Dark Ages. It marks the
turn of the tide of barbarism in the seventh and eighth
centuries. It infused new life into the continental Church
and the decadent classical civilization and was one of
the main formative influences in the development of
Carolingian culture. Nevertheless it was not destined
to endure. It was gradually superseded by the Carolingian culture which it had done so much to create,
and mediaeval culture as a whole is based not on the
Christian-vernacular tradition of the Irish and the
Anglo-Saxons, but on the Carolingian-Latin tradition that superseded it.

In England the Anglo-Saxon culture gradually
came under the sway of continental influences, until
it was finally incorporated in the unity of western

continental culture as a result of the Norman Conquest. In Ireland, on the other hand, the old tradition
of vernacular culture was too strong to be forcibly
uprooted and it preserved its identity and continuity
unbroken through the Viking and Anglo-Norman
invasions. But in consequence Celtic Ireland lost touch
with the rest of Western Christendom and was isolated
from the dominant current of mediaeval culture to
such an extent that by the twelfth century St Bernard
can write of the old pioneer of Christian learning as an
outer land of barbarism and semi-paganism.

No doubt the ravages of the Viking invasions were
largely responsible for the decline of the insular cultures, but the fundamental cause of the change was the
divergence between continental and insular civilization that followed the rise of the Carolingian empire.
Both of them were founded on the culture of the
Church and the monasteries, both looked back to the
patristic and classical tradition; but while in the British Isles these traditions were fused with those of the
native vernacular culture, on the continent they united
with the tradition of the Christian Empire to form an
international ecclesiastical Latin culture which was
common to France and Germany and North Italy, and
gradually extended its influence westward to the British Isles, northward to Scandinavia and eastwards to
Bohemia and the Slavonic borderlands.

III

IT was on the foundation of this Latin-Carolingian
culture rather than on that of the old vernacular literary

tradition that the new vernacular literature of mediaeval Europe was finally developed in the eleventh and
twelfth centuries. It is true that this was not realized by
nineteenth-century scholars, who looked for its origins
in a lost epic tradition which would bridge the gap between the *Chansons de Geste* and the old Teutonic heroic poetry and the national epics of the Franks. But as
Prof. Bédier has shown, this is an *a priori* hypothesis
that has no basis in facts. The *Chansons de Geste* have no
links with the old Frankish national literature. They
grew up in the age of the crusades around the shrines of
the great abbeys, along the pilgrimage roads that led to
Spain. Their models were not the old Germanic epic,
but the new vernacular versions of the Latin legends of
the saints like the *Vie de St Foy* and the *Vie de St Alexis*.

Nevertheless, in spite of the errors of the nineteenth-
century view, it contains, as is so often the case with
mistaken theories, an important element of truth. For
though the mediaeval epic is a new creation of the new
culture of Latin Christendom and not the direct descendant of the Germanic national epic, there is a certain continuity, both spiritual and sociological, between these two traditions. The feudal noble was in a
real sense the descendant of the barbarian warrior. He
inherited his social traditions and spiritual ideals. His
moral standards were those of the heroic age—of Beowulf and Hildebrand and the Nibelungs—the fidelity
of the tribal warrior to his chieftain and his kin, the
bloodstained law of private vengeance and family
feud, the ideals of honour and contempt of death and
boundless liberality. During the Dark Ages these
standards and ideals stood in sharp contrast to those of

the Christian tradition, as embodied in the Church and the monastic life. The virtues of the warrior were vices to the monk, and the virtues of the monk were the vices of the warrior. But in the new vernacular literature this dualism of tradition begins to disappear. The heroic type is partially Christianized, and the barbarian warrior becomes the mediaeval knight. The heroes of the *Chansons de Geste* are still bloodthirsty barbarians; they still hold to the law of vengeance and feud; but they are now conscious of a higher loyalty and a new religious conception of Christian heroism.

Thus in the *Song of Roland*, for example, we see the old heroic tradition in the process of transformation under the influence of new religious ideals. Turpin, the warrior archbishop, stands side by side with Roland and Oliver as one of the central figures in the poem, and his sermon to the Franks before the battle is a faithful expression of the union of heroic and Christian elements that went to make up the Crusading ideal.

> "My lord barons, Charles left us here for this;
> He is our king, well may we die for him;
> To Christendom good service offering.
> Battle you'll have, you all are bound to it.
> For with your eyes you see the Sarrazins,
> Pray for God's grace, confessing Him your sins!
> For your souls' health, I'll absolution give,
> So though you die, blest martyrs shall you live,
> Thrones you shall win in the great Paradise."[1]

[1] The *Song of Roland*, trans. C. Scott Moncrieff (1919), 1127-1135.

Above all, as Professor Faral has pointed out,[2] in the cycle of Doon of Mayence—the Song of Raoul of Cambrai, and the rest—we find a remarkable attempt to bring out the conflict and opposition between the two elements in the tradition of the feudal warrior, the law of fidelity and the law of vengeance, destructive barbarism and Christian heroism, pride and obedience. Each of the poems in this cycle centres in an act of rebellion and vengeance, followed by a long sequel of violence and outrage and ending in an act of humility and repentance. Thus Ogier, the Dane, dies in the habit of a monk, Renaud of Montauban works as a labourer among the masons of the Church of St Peter at Cologne, and Ybert of Ribemont in *Raoul of Cambrai* builds seven churches as monuments of his humility on the site of the seven castles that were the monuments of his pride.

Thus there is a genuine religious element in the mediaeval French epic which is all the more striking on account of the background of ferocity and barbarism against which it stands out. For the *Chanson de Geste*, to a far greater extent than either the old heroic epic of the type of Beowulf or the later mediaeval romance, is entirely devoid of all literary sophistication and gives a faithful reflection of the mind of feudal society. It is the literature of the camp as opposed to the literature of the school.

For we must not forget that the age of the *Chansons de Geste* was also the great age of mediaeval humanism and classical scholarship, when cultivated men of letters like Hildebert of Lavardin, Baudri of Bourgeuil, Marbod of Rennes and John of Salisbury

[2] In Bédier et Hazard, *Histoire de la Littérature Française*, I, 14.

modelled their style on Ovid and Cicero, and exchanged scholarly epigrams and epistles like the humanists of a later age. Such men seem to belong to a different tradition, and indeed to a different world from that of the jongleurs who sang of the bloody deeds of their barbarous heroes to men whose only interests were in war, and the contrast makes us realize the dualism which underlay early mediaeval culture and how great a gap had to be bridged before the churchman and the feudal warrior could meet on a common ground of Christian culture. It is true that the new social and economic conditions that began to develop in the eleventh century tended to raise the level of secular culture and to tame the barbarism of feudal society. But it does not necessarily follow that as society grew less barbarous it would grow more Christian. On the contrary, the new conditions favoured the development of new ideals that were to some extent incompatible with Christian standards, and it seemed possible that feudal society might pass direct from the paganism of barbarism to an even more pagan culture.

IV

FOR as a matter of fact the literary development which was to transform the standards of feudal society and to create the new vernacular poetry and the new secular culture, had its origins neither in the Latin Christian culture of the Church, nor in the heroic tradition of northern feudalism. It was an exotic growth which arose in southern France under the shadow of the brilliant and advanced Moslem culture of Spain and the western Mediterranean to which it probably owed some of its most distinctive features. It shows itself not only in a new style of poetry but in new forms of social life and new ideals of moral conduct. It created the new attitude to woman, the new cult of romantic love and the new ideals of courtesy and chivalry that did so much to transform mediaeval culture that they now appear almost inseparable from it. Yet it has no roots in the older mediaeval past. It is neither Christian nor Germanic, and it has no contact with the heroic epic tradition which had hitherto been the inspiration of Western vernacular literature.

Nothing, in fact, could be more mistaken than the old view which derives the poetry of the troubadours and the new ideals that are associated with it from the influence of Christian idealism or northern feudalism. We see that influence in the *Chansons de Geste*, but it finds expression not in the cult of woman and of romantic love, but in the exaltation of the heroic virtues and of the ideals of the crusade. But even this modicum of Christian influence is lacking in the new poetry of the South. It is not without its own idealism and its moral code, but they are not those of Christianity. Its outlook is entirely this-worldly, and is equally opposed to the asceticism of mediaeval Christianity and to the barbaric simplicity of the northern tradition. It finds expression above all in the cult of woman and the romantic ideal of love and in the elaborate code of courtesy and chivalrous behaviour, which is at once so rigid and so antinomian. (That Faith Frees One From The Obligations of The Moral Law)

This new literary movement, and the culture of

which it was the expression, spread with extraordinary rapidity through Western Europe in the second
half of the twelfth century. Its chief centre of diffusion was the Angevin court, where Eleanor of
Aquitaine, the grand-daughter of the first of the troubadours, was its great patron; while her daughters,
Marie of Champagne and Mathilda of Saxony, and her
niece, Elizabeth of Vermandois, the Countess of
Flanders, also took a leading part in the work of diffusion. It was in these circles that there arose the new
courtly epic which grafted the ideas and motives of the
courtly literature of the south on to the northern legendary stock, thus producing the romances of Tristan
and Lancelot and the rest of the Arthurian cycle, which
gradually took the place of the *Chansons de Geste* as the
standard literature of feudal society.

This was in a sense a victory for culture over barbarism, since it taught the feudal nobility of Northern
Europe new standards of social intercourse and civilized behaviour. The brutal violence of the barbarian
warrior, which appears no less plainly in the heroes of
the *Chansons de Geste* than in those of the Nordic Sagas,
gradually yielded to the new ideals of honour and
courtesy and the service of ladies. But from the religious point of view there was no such progress. The
new spirit was not merely non-religious, it was potentially unorthodox and anti-clerical. It is no accident
that the cradle of the courtly literature and culture
should also have been the centre of the Albigensian
heresy and the first country in western Europe to revolt against the religious unity of Christendom. Nothing, it is true, could seem more dissimilar at first sight

from the 'joyful wisdom' of the troubadours than the world-refusing asceticism of the Catharists. Nevertheless they are in a sense parallel phenomena. Both of them were exotic growths which had no roots in Christian culture, but which found a favourable soil in the brilliant and precocious society of Languedoc. Moreover our knowledge of mediaeval Catharism is too scanty for us to be able to trace its relations to contemporary literature, and I do not think that we can entirely exclude the possibility of the existence of an esoteric and unorthodox tradition in courtly literature, such as the late Luigi Valli maintained in his ingenious and often extravagant theories on the secret language of Dante and the *Fedeli d'Amore*.[3] Certainly the centres of the new poetry both in Southern France and Southern Italy were also the centres of disaffection to the Church, and the philosophy that underlies the erotic mysticism of the *dolce stil nuovo* in Tuscany owed more to the speculations of the Averroists and to Islamic mysticism than to the orthodox tradition of Western scholasticism.

v

IT is a sign of the vitality and cultural influence of mediaeval religion that it succeeded in assimilating this new literary tradition, and making it the instrument of its own spiritual ideals.

Instead of secularizing mediaeval culture, the court-

[3] Valli, *Il Linguaggio Segreto di Dante e dei Fedeli d'Amore*, Rome, 1928.

ly tradition itself became Christianized. We see this above all in the development of the mediaeval tradition of chivalry. That tradition had its origins in the military institutions and ideals of the feudal warrior caste. It acquired from the courtly tradition of the south a code of manners and a common type of culture which transformed the knight from a mere fighting man into a gentleman and a man of the world. But mediaeval chivalry at its best was something much more than this. It was a sacred institution consecrated by religious rites and dedicated to the service of God and the defence of Holy Church.

This religious conception of chivalry is already implicit in the crusading movement; it finds explicit expression in the new military orders, whose ideals were set forth by St Bernard himself in his work *In praise of the New Knighthood*, and finally in the thirteenth century it becomes organically united with the classical institutions of mediaeval knighthood as shown in the religious ceremonies by which a knight was created and the religious character of the engagements which he swore to observe.

Now this same process of development is reflected in the literature of feudal society and in the evolution of mediaeval epic. The *Chansons de Geste* represent, as we have seen, the barbaric heroism of northern feudalism already coloured in some degree by Christian ideals. The development of the romantic epic by Chrétien de Troyes and the authors of *Tristan* marks the introduction of the new courtly literature into the north and the development of new forms of secular culture. But this new literature, whether in its epic or lyrical forms, lacks the religious inspiration which the *Chansons de Geste*, for all their rudeness, undoubtedly possess. It is an exotic and artificial development which has no contact with the deeper elements in the western soul. Consequently we find in the thirteenth century a deliberate attempt to moralize the courtly tradition and to infuse an element of religious idealism into the secular romanticism of the courtly epic. The result of this is to be seen in the romantic mysticism of the Grail legend, above all in the great prose cycle of *Lancelot del Lac*,[4] which was composed, probably under Cistercian influence, in the first quarter of the thirteenth century, between 1220 and 1225. Here the whole material of Arthurian romance is remoulded in accordance with the religious conception of chivalry, and the courtly motive of romantic love is subordinated to the religious allegory of the quest for the Grail, the symbol of spiritual vision.

The same tendency to spiritualize the courtly epic by the infusion of a religious motive is to be found in Germany in the Parsifal of Wolfom von Eschenbach, while even the courtly lyric, which in France retained its secular character to the end, acquires in the work of Walter von der Vogelweide a new depth of thought and religious feeling which raises it far above the formal artificiality of the great bulk of courtly poetry,

---

[4] This is a trilogy, consisting of three parts, the Book of Lancelot, The Quest of the Holy Grail, and the Morte d'Arthur. I follow the view of Prof. F. Lot—*Étude sur le Lancelot en prose* (1918)—in ascribing the whole trilogy to a single author, but opinions differ on this subject, and some scholars regard it as a composite work.

whether Provençal or French. It is indeed a remarkable fact that this moralization of the courtly tradition by the introduction of religious motives represents in each of the cases we have mentioned a distinct gain from the literary point of view. In post-Renaissance literature this is rarely the case; the literature of edification is usually bad literature, and the attempt to give a good story a good moral is usually fatal to both. Yet in the case of the Arthurian legend, we find the author of the prose *Lancelot* ruthlessly recasting a series of romantic tales of love and adventure in the interests of religion and morals and making a triumphant success of it, since the introduction of the religious motive gives the whole cycle an artistic unity and a spiritual significance that it had never before possessed.

VI

THUS we see how the courtly tradition, in spite of its purely secular origins and its somewhat antinomian tendencies, was gradually brought into relation with religious thought and incorporated in the spiritual unity of mediaeval Christendom. It is true that the literature of chivalry is so remote from real life that it is difficult to draw definite conclusions from it with regard to mediaeval culture. Far more significant is the evidence of the new vernacular religious literature that makes its appearance in the thirteenth century, for this is perhaps the most vital and spontaneous expression of the mediaeval mind. And the characteristic feature of this literature is its use of the forms and ideas of the courtly tradition to express religious experience,—the transformation of romanticism into mysticism and of chivalry into religious devotion.

The root of this development is to be found in St Francis, who had an instinctive attraction to the romantici dealism of the courtly literature. Unlike the other great religious leaders of the Middle Ages, St Francis was a stranger to the Latin traditions of ecclesiastical culture; he belonged to the new world of the Italian city states, a world that was already outgrowing the semi-Byzantine traditions of the older Italy, but which had not yet begun to realize the new forms of social life and secular culture that were to find expression in the age of the Renaissance. We see from the vernacular literature of the following century—for example in the sonnets of Folgore of San Gemignano—how the aristocratic society of the new commercial cities adopted the fashions of the feudal courts and strove to outdo them in magnificence and display, and in the same way St Francis himself in his youth was dazzled and attracted by the ideals of courtly chivalry that were then entering the Italian peninsula from across the Alps.

Now his conversion, so far from causing him to abandon these ideals for the traditional monastic asceticism, gave them a new significance which inspired his whole religious mission. The ideals of his fraternity were founded on those of romantic chivalry rather than on those of Benedictine monasticism. It was to be an order of spiritual knighthood, dedicated to the service of the Cross and the love of the Lady Poverty. The friars were his 'Brethren of the Round Table', 'jongleurs of God', and they were to set forth

like Knight Adventurers on the path of God, perform-
ing deeds of spiritual prowess, shrinking from no hardship or danger and finding their reward in the service
of love. Thus the courtly ideals of courtesy, joy, generosity and romantic love found a new religious application of which the life of St Francis himself was the perfect manifestation and which already appears in literary form in the writings of the early Franciscans, above
all in the *Sacrum Commercium*, which describes the woo-
ing of the Lady Poverty by St Francis in the form of a
symbolic romance.

In the course of the thirteenth century, this religious
adaptation of courtly literature and chivalrous idealism spread—whether by Franciscan influence or by a
spontaneous development—from one end of Christendom to the other. One of the earliest and most perfect
examples is to be found in Flanders, in the writings of
the obscure Béguine, Hadewych, who composed her
vernacular mystical poems entirely in the form and
spirit of the courtly lyric about the middle of the
thirteenth century. Another example of the same period is the famous German mystic, Mechtild of Magdeburg. In Italy we have the great Franciscan poet, Jacopone da Todi; while perhaps the most complete and
elaborate development of the tendency is to be found in
the writings of the great Catalonian mystic Ramon
Lull, above all in his great mystical romance of *Blan-
querna*, and in the *Book of the Lover and the Beloved*, in
which the influence of Islamic literature and Islamic
mysticism is plainly visible. This literature is of ex-
ceptional interest to the student of mediaeval religion,
since in it are to be found the beginnings of the great

mystical movement which reached its full development in the fourteenth century and which we have discussed in a previous chapter. For while that movement was on the one side learned and speculative, based on the metaphysics of the Dominican schoolmen and on the Christian Neoplatonism of the Pseudo-Dionysius, on the other hand it was connected with the vernacular tradition of secular culture and with the popular appeal of the Franciscan spirit. Both these elements already exist side by side in the writings of Jacopone da Todi and Ramon Lull, and we find them reappearing in the full tide of fourteenth-century Dominican German mysticism with Henry Suso, who embodied the tradition of Eckhart in the forms of the courtly literature. Moreover at the same time we find this transformed courtly tradition, at once spiritualized and popularized, as an important element in the formation of the new vernacular poetry which was making its appearance in England.

VII

BUT the influence of mediaeval religion on the literary tradition of the courtly culture does not only show itself in the adaptation of this tradition to the service of vernacular mysticism and popular piety; it also plays an essential part in the formation of the greatest literary genius of the Middle Ages. Dante's earlier poetry is the crown and consummation of the courtly tradition in its most mature and exquisite form, and even in the *Divina Commedia* he still acknowledges his debt to the

masters of Provençal and Italian courtly poetry, Arnaut
Daniel and Guido Guincelli. Nevertheless, as Dante's
genius ripens, it transcends the limits of the courtly
tradition and becomes at once more classical and more
Christian. The Lady of the *Convivio* and perhaps also
the Beatrice of the *Vita Nuova* belong to the strange
twilight world in which the abstractions of Averroistic
metaphysics are clothed in the forms of Provençal love
poetry, and the return of Dante from the strange lady
of the *Convivio* to the heavenly Beatrice of the *Divina
Commedia* marks the progress of his thought back from
the exotic half-oriental world of the courtly poets to
the central tradition of Christian culture. It is Virgil,
the representative of the classical tradition, who is
Dante's leader in this spiritual pilgrimage, and it is in
him, rather than in Guido Guincelli or Arnaut Daniel
that Dante recognizes his true master.

> *Tu se' lo mio maestro e il mio autore,*
> *Tu se solo colui, da cui io tolsi*
> *Lo bello stilo che m'ha fatto honore.*

> "Thou art my master and my author thou,
> Thou art alone the one from whom I took
> The beautiful style that has done honour to me."

Thus Dante's great poem represents the achievement of a final synthesis of the literary and the religious traditions of the Middle Ages, a synthesis that embodies all the vital elements of mediaeval culture.
Christian theology and the science and philosophy of
the Arabs, the courtly culture of the troubadours and the
classical tradition of Virgil, the mysticism of Dionysius

and the piety of St Bernard, the Franciscan spirit of reform and the Roman order, Italian national feeling and Christian universalism—all find their place in the organic structure of the poet's thought and in the artistic unity of his work. Yet at the same time the *Divina Commedia* also faithfully reflects the crisis of the later Middle Ages and the failure of mediaeval Christendom to overcome the centrifugal forces that were about to destroy its unity. It is true that Dante still stands for the ideal of Catholic universalism against the territorial and ecclesiastical self-assertion of the new national monarchies. But he no longer looks to the Papacy as the representative of Christian universalism and the leader of the movement of Catholic reform. The Papacy had itself become compromised in his eyes by secularism and by its subservience to the French monarchy. And consequently it is to the Empire rather than to the Papacy that he looks for the realization of a universal Christian order and the delivery of the Church from its state of bondage.

But Dante's ideal of the Empire no longer has any relations with history and reality. His emperor is not the real Henry VII, but an apocalyptic figure, the Messianic DVX whose coming he foretells in a strain of prophetic inspiration in the great vision of the Earthly Paradise in the concluding cantos of the *Purgatorio*. But the Prince who was actually to come was a very different figure, it was the Prince of Macchiavelli who was, after all, the lineal descendant of the Can Grandes and the Castruccio Castrucanis in whom Dante had put his trust. Thus Dante's conception of a world state which should be the perfect embodiment

of *humana civilitas*, and should actualize all the potentialities of human nature, had no relations to political
reality or to the historical facts of his age. It is the last
glimpse of that vision of spiritual unity which had inspired the mediaeval mind for nine hundred years, and
had guided the development of mediaeval culture from
its beginnings in the age of St Augustine and Prudentius, through the age of Alcuin and Charles the Great,
of Nicholas I and Otto III, to its final and yet incomplete
realization in thirteenth-century Christendom.

An incomplete realization, I have said, for on the
one hand no society or culture has ever realized the
aspirations of its greatest minds, and, on the other, the
Christian ideal most of all tends to transcend all cultural
forms. Nevertheless there has never been an age in
which Christianity attained so complete a cultural expression as in the thirteenth century. Europe has seen
no greater Christian hero than St Francis, no greater
Christian philosopher than St Thomas, no greater
Christian poet than Dante, perhaps even no greater
Christian ruler than St Louis.

I do not maintain that the general level of religious
life was higher than at other times or that the state of
the Church was healthier, still less that scandals were
rarer or moral evils less obvious. What one can assert
is that in the Middle Ages more than at other periods
in the life of our civilization, the European culture
and the Christian religion were in a state of communion: the highest expressions of mediaeval culture, whether in art, in literature or in philosophy,
were religious and the greatest representatives of mediaeval religion were also the leaders of mediaeval cul-

ture. This is not, of course, an inevitable state of things. It may even be argued that the dualism of religion and culture that existed under the Roman Empire, and more or less generally in modern times, is the normal condition of Christianity. Nevertheless the other alternative, that of a co-operation and collaboration between religion and culture, is undoubtedly a more ideal system, and from this point of view the mediaeval achievement remains unsurpassed by any other age.

THE ORIGINS OF THE ROMANTIC
TRADITION

THE quarrel between Romanticism and Classicism has caused more ink to be spilt than any other literary controversy, even that of the Ancients and the Moderns, and after more than a century of warfare matters stand very much where they were at the beginning. Goethe's famous definition "Classicism is health, Romanticism is disease" is typical of the sweeping generalizations on which the controversy has thrived. For each party has identified its enemy with anything that it despised in literature, and there has been little attempt to arrive at a common basis of definition. Moreover, the controversy has been embittered by the introduction of religious and political issues, and in our days it has become not so much a literary controversy as a heresy hunt conducted with inquisitorial rigour by Ernest Seillière or, with Professor Babbitt, a crusade for the moral regeneration of society.

The fact is that Romanticism has become a label for half a dozen different things, that have only an accidental connection with one another. We may, perhaps, be justified in giving the name to that great change in taste and feeling that passed over Europe at the beginning of the nineteenth century; but strictly speaking Romanticism is only one element in that change. The term originally possessed a perfectly simple and objective meaning, and though it may be pedantic to confine it to that meaning, it is at least desirable not to lose sight of it altogether. That meaning is very clearly defined by Mme de Stael, who, I believe, was the first to introduce the word into French literature. "The term 'romantic'," she writes, "has recently been introduced in Germany to designate the poetry that had its origin in the songs of the troubadours, that which was born of Christianity and Chivalry . . . The word 'classic' is sometimes taken as synonymous with perfection. I use it here in another sense, regarding classical poetry as that of the ancients, and romantic poetry as that which is in some way connected with the institutions of chivalry."

This in fact is a perfectly logical and satisfactory definition. Romanticism is the literary imitation of the mediaeval romances, as classicism is the imitation of the Latin Classics; and just as the Renaissance meant the return to classical antiquity and the revival of classical literature, so the Romantic Revival had its origin in the return to the Middle Ages and the revival of mediaeval literature. No doubt the Romantic movement met and mingled with that other movement of return to nature and sentiment that has its origin with Rousseau. But the two are no more to be identified with one another than the Renaissance is to be identified with the Reformation. Indeed the relation between Humanism and Protestantism affords a very fair parallel to that between Romanticism and Rousseauism. The rediscovery of the Middle Ages by the Romantics is an event of no less importance in the history of European thought than the rediscovery of Hellenism by the Humanists. It meant an immense widening of our intellectual horizon. To Boileau and Pope and their contemporaries the Middle Ages were simply a gap in the history of culture. They had no eyes for the beauty of mediaeval art and no ears for the melody of mediaeval verse. All this was restored to us by the Romantics. They went to the Middle Ages not in order to prove a case or to justify their political or religious beliefs, but because they found in them something utterly different from the world that they knew—the revelation of a new kind of beauty. Was this but another example of the romantic fallacy that what is far away must be finer and more beautiful than what is near at hand and that human nature was different in the past to what it is in the present? I do not think so. I believe that the discovery of the Romantics was a genuine discovery and that there really is something in mediaeval culture essentially different from anything that is to be found either in the ancient or the modern world, and that we can never understand mediaeval history unless we discover what it is.

And if we wish to find this mysterious element which is the quintessence of the mediaeval spirit we cannot do better than to follow the example of the Romantics and look for it in the age and the country of the Troubadours, for it is there that we shall find it purest and least alloyed. Elsewhere mediaeval life differs from our own mainly by its more primitive character; it is, in fact, the ancestral form of our own culture. The predominance of the religious element may at first sight seem strange to us, but after all religion is always with us, and the emotions and thoughts of a religious man in the Middle Ages do not differ essentially from those of a religious man to-day. But in the world of the Troubadours it is the whole pattern of life and thought that is different. They differ from ourselves not so much because they are less civilized but because they are civilized in a different way, and there is no standard of comparison by which the two cultures can be judged.

The men of Provence and Languedoc were warriors
and politicians, but they do not live by their political
achievements, nor yet by their economic achievements
though they were also great merchant adventurers.
Their supreme title to fame is their art of life—whether
it be *el gay saber*—the joyful science of poetry and love
in the technical sense, or the general standard of aristocratic behaviour which inspired their social life.

For it was the Provençal culture which created those
new ideals and conventions of courtesy and chivalry
and romantic love that were gradually transmitted to
the other countries of Western Europe and that transformed the whole life and thought of aristocratic
society. The significance of this element in mediaeval
culture is missed alike by those who regard the Middle
Ages as a time when life was darkened and narrowed
by superstition and asceticism, and by those who ideal-
ize them as an age of mystical enthusiasm and high
moral endeavour when all social life was inspired by
the ideals of the Christian faith. To the latter, chivalry
and courtly love seem to show the refining influence of
Christian ideas on manners and morals, while the pes-
simists for their part are quick to seize on the moral
weaknesses of courtly society as a proof of the short-
comings of mediaeval Catholicism.

In reality the ideals of the new culture had nothing
to do with religion, and its practice was immoral not
because it violated accepted standards, but because of
the very nature of the standards themselves. Or rather
one may say that Provençal society possessed an elaborate moral code, but it was not that of Christianity.
Its ideal was a frankly pagan one—the glorification of

life, the assertion of the individual personality and the cultivation of the pleasures of the senses. The supreme ends of life were 'joy and honour', and they were embodied in the cult of woman and the ideal of courtly love which form the stock themes of Provençal literature. The contrast between this ideal and the Christian view of life finds open expression in the following well-known passage from *Aucassin and Nicolette*, a work which in spite of its North French form belongs in spirit entirely to the southern society in which the scene is laid.

"In Paradise what have I to do? I seek not to enter there, but only to have Nicolette my most sweet friend, whom I so love. For into Paradise go none but such folk as I shall tell you. There go these old priests and the old cripples and the maimed who all day and all night crouch in front of the altars and in the old crypts and those who are clad in old worn-out coats and tattered rags, who go naked and barefoot and full of sores, who die of hunger and hardship and cold and wretchedness. All these go into Paradise, with these I have nothing to do. But into Hell I am willing to go; for to Hell go the fine clerks and the fair knights who have fallen in jousts and in ripe wars and the skilled warriors and the brave men. With them I am fain to go. There also go the fair and courteous ladies who have two lovers or three and their own lords beside. And there go the gold and the silver and the ermines and the grey furs; there too the harpers and the rhymers and the kings of the world. With these will I go too, so that I may have with me Nicolette, my most sweet friend."[1]

[1] Trans. Laurence Housman (1902), p. 13.

But perhaps this open disavowal of Christian ideals is less characteristic than the complete ignoring of them which we find in a Provençal romance like *Flamenca* where the hero uses the most sacred rites of religion in order to gain the love of a married woman without the slightest scruple or sense of moral incongruity.

These examples may perhaps be ascribed to the naive immoralism of the mediaeval romantic tradition, but there is certainly nothing naive about the Provençal literature as a whole. It has its roots not in the traditions of the folk-song and the life of the people but in a highly refined and sophisticated literary tradition.

The art of the troubadours is in fact the starting point of modern European literature. As W. P. Ker wrote: "Everything that is commonly called poetry in the modern tongues may in some way or other trace its pedigree back to William count of Poitou, 'the first of a school that includes every modern poet'. It is a different thing with the verse of the old Teutonic school. It is possible to understand it but in spite of blood relationship its character is strange . . . the form is not that of the modern world. But the relations of the Provençal school are everywhere and they can be proved by historical evidence without any hazardous speculation on poetical affinities. They include all sorts and degrees of poets. By contrast with what precedes 1100, the whole of modern poetry since then appears one community."[2]

How are we to explain the abrupt appearance of this new literary art and the new secular culture that produced it? The accepted explanation has been that they are the natural flowering of the northern chivalrous

[2] W. P. Ker, *The Dark Ages*, pp. 6 and 8-9.

spirit—the Gothic genius—which developed precoci-
ously in the forcing-house of the Mediterranean lands.
Thus according to Vossler, "the first who espoused the
cause of the fair sex and set rolling, as it were, the eman-
cipation of woman were knights. The noble lords north
of the Alps had remained true to the old German feeling
of the frank acceptance and enjoyment of the good
things of life."[3]

In reality, however, the new ideals of love and courtesy make their first appearance in Northern Europe
only in consequence of and in proportion to the recep-
tion of Provençal influences. Even in French literature,
which is nearest to that of Languedoc, there is no trace
of an independent development of the ideals of courtesy and romantic love. The behaviour of the heroes of
the *Chansons de Geste* towards women is very much
that of the cave man and their language is often as frank
as a bargee's. Their idealism is to be found not in their
attitude to woman but in their religious patriotism—
that spirit of crusading energy which is so nobly expressed in the *Song of Roland*. But as soon as we turn to
the poetry of the troubadours we find ourselves in a
completely different world. Instead of the magnificent
simplicity of the *chansons* with their clanging assonance
like the tramp of armed men, we have the delicate and
difficult music of the Provençal lyric which aims at the
same ideal of civilized perfection as the Petrarchan sonnet.

And the change in spirit and feeling is even more
striking. In contrast to the objective and anonymous
simplicity of the French epic poet, the troubadour is

[3] Vossler, *Mediaeval Culture*, I, 299.

absorbed in the study of his own emotions and has already acquired a passion for psychological analysis. But this does not lead them to romantic sentimentality as we might expect. The greatest of them, men such as Peire d'Auvergne and Arnaut Daniel, express the morbid intensity of their passion with an austere reticence which gives their poetry an almost classical character, as in the lines of the former:

> Why doth she ask me naught? That grieveth me,
> Yet fear lest I not better fare but worse;
> The more the pain I say 'So let it be'.

They pride themselves not so much on the obvious appeal of thought and expression as on an obscure and difficult beauty—*chantar ab motz serratz e clus*—and when there were two ways of saying a thing they always preferred the most difficult. It is the spirit of Arnaut Daniel's famous boast:

> I am Arnaut who gathers air
> And with the oxen chase the hare
> And ever swim against the stream.

Compare on the one hand a passage from the *Song of Roland*:

> The count Rolanz has never loved cowards
> Nor arrogant nor men of evil heart
> Nor chevalier that was not good vassal.
> That Archbishop, Turpins, he calls apart:
> 'Sir, you're afoot and I my charger have;
> For love of you here will I take my stand,
> Together we'll endure things good and bad,

I'll leave you not for no incarnate man:
We'll give again these pagans their attack;
The better blows are those from Durendal.'[4]

And on the other hand these lines of Arnaut Daniel:

Only I know what over-anguish falls
Upon the love-worn heart from over-love,
Because of my desire so firm and whole
Toward her I loved on sight and since alway,
Which turneth not aside nor wavereth;
So far from her I speak for her mad speech
Who near her, for o'er much to speak, am dumb.[5]

In the one case the warlike simplicity of the thought is
matched by the ringing monotony of the assonance.
In the other there is no rhyme within the stanza, but the
seven several rhymes are carried over and repeated in
the same order six times with a concluding refrain of
the last three. As Ezra Pound says, it is one of the most
musical arrangements of words in sequence whereof
we know, for it satisfies "not only the modern ear
gluttonous of rhyme but also the ear trained to Roman
and Hellenic music to which rhyme seemed and seems
a vulgarity."[6]

The two styles are practically contemporary, and
both of them developed on French or rather Gallic soil,
yet in spite of this they are as different from one another
in form and content as any two literatures well can be.
There is nothing save the name in common between

[4] Trans. C. S. Scott-Moncrieff, lines 2134-2143.
[5] Trans. E. Pound in *The Spirit of Romance*, p. 18.
[6] *Op. cit.*, p. 13.

the rude Christian chivalry of the north and the refined secular courtly chivalry of the South. And if the French epic expresses, as it surely does, the northern 'Gothic' spirit of the Christianized barbarian warrior, then we must look elsewhere for the sources of the Provençal literature. One might have supposed that the persistence of the classical tradition in the old Roman *provincia,* the most Latinized region north of the Alps, might provide an explanation. But though some of the troubadours, such as Arnaut Daniel, were not without the rudiments of Latin culture, there is obviously no direct connection between Provençal and Latin poetry. It was actually in the North, in the valleys of the Loire and the Meuse and the Rhine, that the influence of the classical tradition asserted itself most strongly and that the mediaeval revival of Latin literature took place. There were no Latin scholars in Provence to compare with those of Chartres and Tours and Liège in the eleventh and twelfth centuries, and while the schools of the North were returning to Cicero and Ovid, the chief centre of studies in Languedoc—Montpellier—was chiefly renowned for the study of the oriental sciences of medicine and astronomy.

And this fact, unimportant as it is for Provençal literature, does actually suggest an answer to the problem. For Provence was not then, as at the present day, in the middle of the European culture area, it was a border territory on the frontier of the oriental world. We are so accustomed to regarding our culture as essentially Western, that it is difficult to remember that there was a time when the most civilized regions of Western Europe belonged to an alien oriental culture, and the

Mediterranean, the cradle of Latin civilization, was in danger of becoming Arabic.

The eighth century had already seen the Moslem conquest of Spain and the invasion of Aquitaine, but it was not until the ninth that the expansion of the Moslem maritime states drove Christian shipping off the seas and converted the basin of the Western Mediterranean into a Saracen lake. The Arabs occupied all the western islands and even established themselves on the mainland of Italy and Provence, where Fraxinetum was for nearly a century (from 888-975) one of the greatest of their pirate strongholds. Finally, the tenth century saw the rise of the Spanish Khalifate and the development of a brilliant culture and literature both in southern and eastern Spain and in Sicily. Although the culture was purely Arabic, the power of the Khalifs rested largely on the native Spanish population and on the European slaves and mercenaries who formed the Khalif's bodyguard. With the break-up of the Khalifate in the eleventh century this European element gained the predominance, and Moslem Spain fell asunder into the mass of small states and city-republics ruled by Moslem Spaniards, Arabs, Berbers and members of the slave guard. The latter established themselves above all in the trading states of the South East, Valencia, Denia and Almeria, and in the Balearic Islands.

But in spite of their political weaknesses these little states were centres of a brilliant court life and of intense literary activity. Rulers like Al Mu'tamid of Seville and Omar Al Mutawakkil of Badajoz were not only generous patrons of culture but were themselves scholars and poets. At a time when the rest of Western Europe was just emerging from the depths of barbarism, the culture of Moslem Spain had attained complete maturity, and surpassed even the civilizations of the East in genius and originality of thought. Southern and eastern Spain was the richest and most populous country in the West. Its cities with their palaces and libraries and public baths were more like those of the Roman Empire than the miserable groups of wooden hovels which were growing up in mediaeval Europe under the shelter of an abbey or a feudal stronghold. In the tenth century Cordova boasted its 200,000 houses, its 900 bath-houses and its workshops which employed 13,000 weavers as well as its armourers and leather-workers, whose work was famous throughout the civilized world.

All this brilliant development of culture is completely ignored by the ordinary student of mediaeval European history. It is as though it were a lost world which had no more to do with the history of our part than the vanished kingdom of Atlantis. And yet, not only did it lie at the very doors of the Christian world, it was actually mingled with it. The frontiers of Christendom and Islam in the early Middle Ages were constantly shifting. The Moslem princes exacted tribute from their Christian neighbours or paid it to them, took them into their service as mercenaries, and married their daughters. There was a large subject population of Moslems in the Christian states of Spain and of Christians in the Moslem ones, and there was far more tolerance and mutual intercourse between the two elements than during the later Middle Ages. The Arragonese court in the eleventh century was largely Arabic in culture and it is said that Pedro I was unable to sign his name except in Arabic. Even the crusading movement which began in the eleventh century did not stop these relations; indeed, it widened the range of southern influence since it first brought the nobles of France and Burgundy and Normandy into contact with Arabic culture. In spite of their barbarism the northern invaders often adapted themselves to the higher culture of the peoples they had conquered, as we see, above all, in Sicily where the Norman kings surrounded themselves with all the luxury of an oriental court and patronized Moslem scholars and poets.

Nowhere was the contact between the two cultures closer than on the shores of the Gulf of Lyons. The County of Barcelona was a kind of bridge between the two worlds. On the one hand it had suzerainty over some of the Moslem communities of Eastern Spain, such as Tarragona and Saragossa, and on the other hand its rulers were allied by marriage with the great houses of Languedoc and Provence and aimed at building up a powerful state which should extend from Valencia to the frontier of Italy. The ports of this region, above all, Barcelona, Montpellier and Marseilles, were in relation with the Moslem trading states of the Balearic Islands and Spain as well as with Africa and the Levant. Indeed, during the twelfth century they were hardly inferior to the Italian cities in the wealth and extent of their trade. Nor were these relations solely commercial. For it was through this region, no less than Sicily and Toledo, that Western Christendom first established contact with Arabic thought. As Duhem has written, "Mar-

seilles and Montpellier were gates widely open to
oriental science," and some of the earliest Latin translations of Arabic scientific works were made at Marseilles, Toulouse, Beziers and Narbonne, as well as at
Barcelona and Tarragona. The numerous Jewish colonies of Provence were renowned for their learning as
well as for their wealth, and Jewish scholars acted as
intermediaries between the Christian and the Islamic
worlds. They were equally at home in France and Spain
and Africa, as we see from the activity of Simon ibn
Tibbon of Lunel who produced his (Hebrew) translations at Arles, Marseilles, Toledo, Barcelona and
Alexandria.

Under these circumstances there seems no inherent
improbability in the view that the rise of the new Provençal culture was affected by the older and more advanced civilization of Western Islam which already
embraced the greater part of the Western Mediterranean area. In fact, this was the solution which first suggested itself to the scholars of the Romantic period
more than a century ago, and its abandonment was due
less to scientific reasons than to the nationalist tendency
to insist on the independent and native origin of Western culture.[7]

[7] This view was current throughout the eighteenth century.
Its chief advocate was the Spanish Jesuit, J. Andres, in his *Origine,
progressi e stato attuale d' ogni letteratura*, 1782-1799. I have not
seen Andres' work, but I believe that he bases his argument not
only on the chivalrous character of the Moorish culture, but
also on specific literary resemblances, such as the occurrence of
the refrain and the monorhyme and the existence of the *tenson*
or poetical debate in Arabic literature. The theory was popularized by Ginguené and Sismondi who derived their views from

Of course, if we assume that the ideals of chivalry and courtesy which ultimately became so characteristic of mediaeval society were of purely native growth, then there is no difficulty in ascribing a similar origin to the rise of the new Provençal literature. But it is just this assumption which is open to criticism. In the tenth century the higher culture of Christian Europe was Latin and ecclesiastical, while the feudal society was still almost barbarian. In Moslem Spain, on the other hand, there existed a rich and brilliant society which had already developed a characteristic type of chivalry. Fighting was not merely the hard and brutal trade of the professional soldiers, it was surrounded by a halo of romance and possessed an elaborate code of conventional etiquette. Horsemanship and the use of arms were fine arts which became the subject of learned treatises and of technical discussion. The exploits of the famous champions were famous throughout Spain and were the theme of poetry and romance.

Moreover, conditions in Spain in the tenth and eleventh centuries were far more favourable than those of northern Europe to the development of courtly society. It was a land of rich cities whose princes strove to outdo one another in the brilliance of their court life and in their munificence towards poets and men of letters.

While the nobility of feudal Europe was almost illi-

Andres. In the last decade of the eighteenth century the Moorish origin of the new poetry was also maintained by Herder, but I do not know whether he reached his conclusions independently of Andres. The opposite theory of Northern and Germanic origin was first clearly stated by Bouterwek in 1801.

terate and the profession of the jongleur or minstrel
was a despised and plebeian occupation, in Islam poetry
was a noble art which even princes were not ashamed
to cultivate. And thus it is in Moslem Spain rather than
in Northern Europe that we must look for the proto-
type of the knightly troubadour whose art was thoroughly aristocratic and who could enter into the spirit
of Al Mutanabbi's famous lines: "I am known to the
horse troop, the night and the desert's expanse; Not
more to the paper and pen than the sword and the
lance." For the most distinctive feature of Spanish culture was its passion for poetry and music, and this passion extended through every rank and class from theologians like Ibn Hazm, philosophers like Ibn Bajja and
statesmen like Al Mutamid to the wandering minstrels
who sang at tournaments or at street corners. An Arab
writer of this age has left a curious description of how
he suffered during an illness at Malaga in 1015 from the
musical propensities of the Spaniards. "All round my
house there was an incessant jangle of singing and of
lutes, tomburs and lyres which disturbed me intensely
and added to the restlessness and suffering caused by
my illness. These toccatas and songs nailed themselves
to my mind without hope of respite, so that I was filled
with aversion for them and would have liked to find a
house away from all the noise, but this was difficult in
Malaga for the people are absolutely dominated by
their passion for music."[8]

The development of Arabic music in Moslem Spain
has recently been studied in detail by Professor Ribera,
who maintains that it affords the key to the interpreta-

[8] Ribera, *Music in Ancient Arabia and Spain*, p. 115.

tion of the new secular music of mediaeval Europe that makes its first appearance with the troubadours. If this is so, it goes a long way towards proving the wider thesis of the debt of Provençal culture to the Moslem world. In any case it is generally acknowledged that the lute, the most popular mediaeval instrument, reached Europe through Spain, and this alone suggests the possibility that the music and prosody of the troubadours was derived from the same source.

There is certainly little resemblance between the classical Arabic poetry with its long metres and its sustained monorhyme and the dancing measures and complex rhyme scheme of the Provençal verse. But in the eleventh century Spanish poetry was no longer confined to the traditional Arabic forms. As in Persia, at the other extremity of the Moslem world, the blending of Arabic and native traditions had produced new literary forms. But while in Persia the typical creation of the period is the *Mathnawi*—the epic, rhymed in couplets—the new development in Spain was essentially lyrical. It produced the new strophic form of verse, the *Zejjel* and the *Muwashshah* or 'girdled' poem —which became extraordinarily popular and spread from Spain to the other parts of the Islamic world. In these new types of verse, each stanza consists of a number of short lines and has its own rhymes, but the Arabic tradition of the monorhyme is preserved in so far that each stanza ends in the same rhyme, which also appears in the refrain. In its simplest form the *Zejjel* consists of a number of quatrains with two rhymes to the stanza (a a a b, c c c b, etc.) but it soon developed an elaborate metrical pattern with multiple internal rhymes. The resemblance between this new type of Arabic poetry and the Provençal lyric is unmistakable. Nor is it easy to explain this resemblance by the theory of a spontaneous parallel evolution, for the Provençal lyric also possesses the monorhyme in the last line of each stanza and in the refrain. This feature is not preserved by the majority of the French and Italian imitators of the Provençal poetry, and it is difficult to explain its origin except as a direct inheritance from Arabic tradition.

And, apart from this point, there is a remarkable resemblance in the general character of the two literatures. Both of them show the same tendency to an elaborate formalism of style which often degenerates into frigid artificiality. Both of them delight in verbal conceits and plays upon words, such as the 'equivocal rhymes' of Arnaut Daniel, where the same words are used in each stanza in a different sense. Moreover, there is considerable resemblance in the main forms of poetry, the love song, the *planh* or lament, the *sirvente* or strife poem and the *tenzon* or poetical debate.

Of these, however, only the last two are at all unusual types and even these may have arisen independently in Provence. But there remains one form which is so completely artificial and unnatural that it can hardly have arisen independently in two cultures during the same period. This is the *descort* of which the alternate lines are each written in a different language. This curious device is well known in Islamic literature, especially in Persia where it is known as the *mulamma* or 'patchwork'. The best known example in mediaeval Christian literature is the Canzone of Dante, *Ai fals ris! per qua traitz avetz*, in which the lines are alternately Provençal, Latin and Italian, but here Dante was only following an established Provençal convention, and the most elaborate example of the type is a descort in five different languages composed by Raimbaut de Vaqueiras in the twelfth century.

But it is not only the external form of Provençal literature which points to Arabic influence. There is an even more remarkable resemblance in the content of the two literatures. As we have seen, the poetry of the troubadours was based upon the cult of woman and the service of the beloved, and it was in Provence that there first arose that ideal of romantic love which inspired the French romances of chivalry, on the one hand, and the *dolce stil nuovo* of Dante and the Italian poets of the Dugento, on the other. Now, there is nothing in the earlier history of mediaeval society to explain this development. The attitude of feudal society towards women, as we see it in the Chansons de Geste and in history, was completely unromantic. Woman was regarded either as a chattel or as the partner of her lord in the management of his fief. Christian morality, especially in its ascetic monastic form, was naturally hostile to and contemptuous of sexual love. Latin erotic poetry certainly existed even in the Dark Ages, but it was based on the tradition of Ovid and was frankly sensual and hedonistic in its conception of love.

But the position in the Islamic world was totally different. The idea of romantic love had existed in Arabic literature from the earliest times and had reached its full development in the tenth century. The misfortunes of lovers and the sorrows of unrequited love are the stock theme of the poet and the story teller and were treated in every imaginable detail. We need look no further than the *Arabian Nights* to realize how widespread and how strong was this romantic tendency. And even in this popular and plebeian form, we cannot but recognize that the attitude to love is not only more romantic but even in a sense more spiritual than anything to be found in Latin literature. Take, for example, the following verses which I quote almost at random:

> I see you with my heart from distant tracts. Do you
> also see me with your heart from afar?
> My heart and my eye are sorrowing for you, my soul
> is with you and you are ever in mind.
> I should not delight in life without seeing you, even
> were I in Paradise or the Garden of Eternity![9]

And if this was to the taste of the street audiences of mediaeval Cairo, what must the attitude of the chivalrous and courtly society of Spain have been in the eleventh century? For in that society woman enjoyed a much higher position than either in modern Islam or in Western Christendom during the Dark Ages. Women were highly educated, especially in calligraphy, music and poetry. There was a considerable number of poetesses, including several of the queens and princesses of the Spanish dynasties. The most famous of these was Wallada, the Ommayyad princess of Cordova, to whom Ibn Zaydun, the greater of the Spanish poets of the eleventh century, devoted his life. His poems ex-

[9] From the story of 'Otbeh and Reyya. Night 680. (Lane's trans.)

press the same spirit of romantic passion and disinterested service which inspired the troubadours and the poets of the *dolce stil nuovo*. Indeed, Von Shack, who rather neglects the Provençal development, declares that it is only in Petrarch that he finds a worthy successor and that his poetry is the earliest expression of the romantic attitude to love and the feeling for nature which characterizes modern literature.[10]

It is, in fact, a great mistake to suppose that there is anything peculiarly Christian or European in the ideal or 'Platonic' conception of love. The love of Beni 'Odhra, the 'children of Chastity' who 'die when they love', had been celebrated by Arab poets from a very early period, and in the tenth century Platonic love had become the subject of elaborate treatises by scholars and theologians.[11] Ibn Hazm, the great Spanish scholar, had written on the subject in the eleventh century and his *Necklace of the Dove* abounds in authentic stories of Spanish Moslems, drawn from all ranks of society, whose love is Platonic and who render silent homage to their beloved and worship her with an almost mystical adoration.[12] At a still later period, at the beginning of the thirteenth century, Ibn 'Arabi, the great Spanish mystic, uses the symbolism of love to express his deepest religious ideas and his book of mystical odes is dedicated to a real lady whom he met at Mecca in 1201 and

[10] Von Shack, *Poesie und Kunst der Araber in Spanien und Sicilien*, I, 280.

[11] Cf. Massignon's description of Ibn Da'ud of Ispanan in his great work on Hallaj the mystic. (Paris, 1922.)

[12] M. Asin, *Islam and the Divine Comedy*, p. 273.

who occupied somewhat the same position in his life as Beatrice did in the life of Dante.[13]

This mystical doctrine of love does not appear in early Provençal literature. In fact, it could not do so, until poetry had come into contact with metaphysical thought, which first occurred in Italy in the thirteenth century. But already in the poems of Arnaut Daniel and the other great troubadours we find the same idealization of the beloved and the same morbid insistence on the frustration of desire which characterized the Arab cult of love in the tenth and eleventh centuries. Moreover, in their treatment of these themes the Provençal poets tend to recur to the same stock motives that we find in the Arabic poetry. For example, one of the stock figures of the Arabic love song, who appears in almost every poem from the earliest times of classical Arabic literature, is the 'slanderer' or 'the talker', and the same figure—'lauzenger', 'lusingatore'—reappears with monotonous regularity in the poetry of the Provençal troubadours and their Italian and German pupils, though it has become a purely formal and often meaningless convention.[14]

Thus there seem to be sufficient grounds not only for admitting an oriental element in Provençal culture but even for regarding the whole movement as due to the spread of the higher civilization of Spain and the Western Mediterranean into southern and south-western France. And there is nothing surprising in this, for the

[13] His book of mystical odes—*Tarjuman al Ashwaq*—has been translated by R. A. Nicholson.

[14] Jeanroy draws attention to the recurrence of these mysterious 'slanderers' (*merkaere, lügenaere*), in the poetry of the German Minnesingers, and uses it as a proof of their dependence on

whole tendency of modern archaeology and culture-history, quite apart from the theories of the extreme diffusionist school, goes to show that the higher culture naturally influences the less advanced ones with which it comes into contact.

Owing to the lack of documentary evidence, it is impossible to say how the process of diffusion took place, though there was, as we have seen, no lack of opportunities for contact between the two cultures. The most obvious channel of communication was through the mixed and often bi-lingual population of north-eastern Spain, and it is quite possible that the jongleurs and minstrels who wandered from court to court in Catalonia and France may have transmitted to the North the music and popular songs of Moslem Spain, since, according to Ribera, the use of the Romance language was not unknown even among the poets of Andalusia.[15] But this does not explain the origin of the thoroughly aristocratic poetry of the troubadours which seems to have first developed not in Catalonia or Provence, but in the Limousin. Even there, however, there was some contact with Spanish culture through the crusades of the eleventh century in which the nobles of that region played a considerable part. Not only did the crusaders become acquainted with the wealth and luxury of Spanish culture, they brought back with them to France Moorish slaves and captives, and in some cases they actually married Moorish women of high position.

Provençal and French models (Jeanroy, *Les Origines de la Poésie lyrique en France*, pp. 283, 289). And the same argument can be applied to its occurrence in Provençal and Arabic poetry.

[15] Ribera, *op. cit.*, p. 120 ff.

When the French crusaders captured Barbastro in
north-east Spain in 1064 each of the principal knights
received a house with all that it contained, women, children and furniture. Ibn Bassam has preserved the report
of a Jewish envoy who was sent to the town to ransom
the daughters of one of the leading citizens. He found
the crusader in Moorish dress seated on a divan surrounded by Moslem girls who were waiting on him.
He refused all the offers of the Jew on the ground that
he had married the daughter of the former owner and
hoped that she would give him descendants. "Her
Moslem ancestors did the same with our women when
they possessed themselves of this country. Now we do
likewise. Thus do we succeed." He then turned to the
girl and in broken Arabic said: "Take your lute and
sing some songs for this gentleman." The Jew adds: "I
was surprised and pleased to see the Count show great
enthusiasm as if he understood the words, though he
continued drinking."[16]

One can well imagine that the French count may
have retained his taste for Arabic music, and that his
children by the Moorish lady might have learned to
compose songs in the Spanish fashion. Actually the
leader of the expedition which captured Barbastro was
the father of the first of the troubadours, William VII
of Poitou, who himself, like so many other troubadours,
took part in the Spanish wars, so that this pasage is one
of the very few pieces of direct evidence that we possess
as to the cultural environment in which the new literature first developed.

In the twelfth century the contact of the troubadours

[16] Ribera, *op. cit.*, pp. 113-4, and Lavisse, *Histoire de France*,

with the Spanish culture is well known. Some of them like Ot de Moncada were themselves of Spanish origin, others like Marcabru spent much of their lives in Spain, while almost all of them had relations with the court of Arragon. Moreover, Provence was also brought into relation with Moslem culture through the eastern crusades in which so many of the troubadours took part and which resulted in the establishment of a Provençal dynasty on the Phoenicean coast.

In the twelfth century Languedoc, particularly the coastal region from Marseilles to Barcelona, possessed wider international contacts and a more cosmopolitan type of culture than any region in Western Europe, apart from the Norman Kingdom of Sicily. This is especially evident in its religious development, in the wealth and culture of its Jewish colonies, which rivalled those of Moslem Spain, and above all, in the prevalence of the heresy of the Catharists which ultimately proved the downfall of the Provençal culture.

For the Albigensian crusade not only uprooted heresy, it also ruined the courtly society in which the art of the troubadours had flourished; in the same way that the French invasions of Italy overwhelmed the brilliant culture of the Italian states in the age of the Renaissance.[17]

II, ii, 86. Ibn Bassam copied the story from Ibn Hayyan the Spanish historian.

[17] The destructive effects of the Albigensian crusade have, however, been absurdly exaggerated. For example, in the *Testament of Beauty* (III, 727-30), Robert Bridges writes as though the whole population was destroyed "and their language wiped out, so that a man to-day reading Provençal song studieth in a dead tongue." Yet the late Poet Laureate can hardly have been ignorant of the existence of Mistral and the Félibrige, even if he

The literature of the thirteenth century is full of lamentations over the passing of Nobility and Honour and Joy—*Paratges, Pretz e Joi*—and the humiliation of 'the courteous folk' before the clerics and the Frenchmen.

There is little evidence that the troubadours showed any active sympathy with the doctrines of the Albigenses. The anticlericalism of poets like Peire Cardenal and Guilhem Figueira has no theological foundation, and the remarkable *Sirvente* of Guilhem Montanhagol against the Inquisition expresses the views not of a Manichaean but of a humanist in revolt against the puritan spirit which condemned the extravagance and display of the courtly society. "The man who despises honour and generosity comes of no good stock, so I hold. For God wills honour and praise, and I know that God made himself true man. And the man who goes against the designs of God, when God has done him the honour to make him in his own image, noble and powerful and nearer to Himself than any creature, such a one is mad if he does not hold himself dear, and behave in this world so that he should have reward hereafter."[18]

But although the culture of the troubadours had no essential connection with the Albigensian heresy, it also had no organic relation to Catholicism. Its roots were in another culture and another spiritual tradition, and when these perished the sources of its own vitality were destroyed. The decline of the Provençal culture

had never heard of the Consistory of the Gay Saber and the Leys d'Amors.

[18] Audiau and Lavaud, *Nouvelle Anthologie des Troubadours*, No. XL.

was but one episode in the general change that passed over the western Mediterranean in the thirteenth century with the fall of the Spanish Moslem culture—a change which was completed by the Angevin conquest of Sicily and the fall of the mixed Siculo-Arab culture of the court of Manfred.

The individualism, the moral laxity and the secular spirit of the troubadours was abhorrent to the religious earnestness and the rigid theological orthodoxy of the new régime, and the poets were forced either to migrate to Arragon and to Italy or to adapt their art to the new conditions. When *el gay saber* was revived in the fourteenth century under the patronage of the University of Toulouse, the Grand Inquisitor, and 'Master Philip surnamed the Elephant', it was a very pale reflection of what it had been in the twelfth century.

Nevertheless, the decay of the Provençal culture did not put an end either to its social or to its literary influence. Its real importance is to be found not so much in its own local and temporary achievement as in the abiding influence that it exercised on European culture. As early as the twelfth century the courtly culture and the new ideal of romantic love had spread to Northern France and thence they gradually penetrated and transformed the spirit of feudal society throughout Europe. Not only did they inspire the new French and German and Iberian poetry which closely follow the forms of Provençal verse, they also blended with the tradition of northern epic and with the Celtic legendary traditions to produce the new cycle of Arthurian romance which had such a vast influence on European literature and sentiment. Here the Provençal ideals of love and courtesy have been brought into relation with the ethical and mystical tradition of mediaeval Catholicism. Nevertheless the union of the two elements did not amount to an organic unity. It retained a certain unreality and moral inconsistency which was afterwards to provoke the pious indignation of Ascham and the profounder criticism of Cervantes. And yet it is just this pursuit of an unattainable unity, this mingling of idealism and sensuality, of chivalry and violence, which constitutes the romantic appeal of the Middle Ages. Where the Christian tradition is completely victorious, as in the case of St Louis, chivalry ceases to be romantic and becomes spiritual and where the other element becomes supreme, as in the court of Burgundy in the fifteenth century, romanticism passes away into gallantry. It is the middle region, the world of Lancelot and Tristan and Thibaut of Champagne, which is the region of romanticism.

It is, however, in Italy that the Provençal tradition attained its highest expression, for there it was not transplanted into an alien culture but developed under similar conditions to those of its native land. In fact, Northern Italy, like Catalonia, was so completely dependent on the Provençal culture that its native poets, such as Sordello and Lanfranco Cigalla, used the Provençal language and are practically indistinguishable from the troubadours of Languedoc, while the culture of Sicily and Apulia, in which the earliest vernacular poetry originated, was even more coloured by oriental influences than that of Provence itself.

Moreover, the new school of Tuscan poetry which

arose in the second half of the thirteenth century, was equally indebted to the Provençal tradition and owes its peculiar character to its union of the art of the troubadours with the thought of Arabic philosophy. The poetry of Guido Cavalcanti and the other poets of the *dolce stil nuovo,* above all the youthful Dante, attains a deeper and more spiritual beauty than anything in the literature of northern chivalry or in that of Provence itself. It is metaphysical poetry in the true sense of the word and it appeals to the intellect no less than to the emotions. Nevertheless it does not altogether overcome the inconsistency which is inherent in the romantic ideal. Its obscurity is due to confusion as well as to profundity of thought. It is an attempt to combine fundamentally dissimilar things, the ideal of the troubadour, the ideal of the Moslem philosopher and the ideal of the Christian mystic.

The Moslems had indeed already succeeded in achieving a synthesis between the first two of these. This synthesis finds its expression in the erotic mysticism of the Sufi poets of Persia and of Arabic writers such as Ibnu'l 'Arabi and Omar Ibnu'l Farid. The latter, for instance, writes:

> Declare the absoluteness of beauty and be not moved
>   to deem it finite by thy longing for a tinselled jewel,
> For the charm of every fair youth or lovely woman
>   is lent to them from Her beauty.
> 'Twas She that crazed Qays the lover of Lubna, ay
>   and every enamoured man like Layla's Majnun or
>   'Azzar's Kutbayyir.
> Every one of them passionately derived Her attribute

which She clothed in the form of a beauty which shone forth in a beauty of form.[19]

This Platonic idealism received a still more elaborate treatment at the hands of the writers of the Spanish school, such as Ibnu'l 'Arabi. They combined it with the metaphysical theory of a series of emanations through which Being and Intelligence descend from God through the celestial spheres and intelligences to the sublunary world, a doctrine which is common to all the Arabic philosophers from Avicenna to Averroes. In accordance with this theory, the Beloved is conceived as the symbol or embodiment of a metaphysical idea. She represents the 'aql—the Universal Intelligence —which is the intermediary between the Divine Unity and the phenomenal world, and the light which illuminates the human mind.

Now it is this idea which was taken over by the Italian poets of the *dolce stil nuovo* and finds typical expression in the Canzoni of Guido Cavalcanti and Dante.[20]

[19]Trans. R. A. Nicholson in *Studies in Islamic Mysticism*, p.222.

[20]The point of contact no doubt is to be found in the Averroistic philosophy which was widely diffused in the West from the time of Michael Scot, but it is possible that the mystical poetry of the type of Ibn'l 'Arabi may also have had some indirect influence. This is the view of Professor Asin and Professor Ribera, and the latter has given as an example the resemblance between the opening stanza of Dante's great canzone, *Tre donne intorno al cor me son venute*, and the well-known Arabic verses about Harun ar Rashid and the three slave girls recorded in the *Kitab ul Agani* of *Al-Isfahani* (tenth century). The parallelism is certainly very striking, but there is not a trace of mysticism in the Arabic original. Still, as Ribera shows, the 'three ladies' became a standard theme of Arabic poetry, and they may well

The lady of the *Convivio* on whom 'every supernal intelligence gazes' and whose 'beauty rains down flames of fire, made living by a gentle spirit which is the creator of every good thought', is neither the Christian Logos, nor a woman of flesh or blood. She is the Averroistic Intelligence that actualizes and illuminates the human mind. Such an idea is quite in harmony with the doctrines of Moslem theology, but it is fundamentally inconsistent alike with the Christian tradition and with the realities of human love. Dante himself was conscious of this when he wrote the sonnet, *Parole Mie*, 'Stay not with her for love is not found there.' And consequently in the great synthesis into which he poured all the wealth of his personal experience and his intellectual inheritance, Christian, Classical and Romantic, this inconsistency is finally transcended. The lady of the *Convivio* is replaced by Virgil, and Beatrice herself becomes a completely Christian figure. And in this synthesis the Provençal element also finds a place. Though Paolo and Francesca, the lovers of romance, are left in Hell, the art of the troubadours, purified and transformed, is admitted into new life. The beautiful and peaceful words of Arnaut Daniel with their echo of his own verse mark the final reconciliation of the art of the troubadours with the classical and the Christian ideals.

> Ieu sui Arnaut que plor e vau cantan
> consiros vei la passada folor
> e vei jausen lo jorn, qu'esper denan.

have been used by Spanish poets of the mystical school whose works have not reached us. Cf. Ribera, *op. cit.*, pp. 162-167.

It is one of the greatest of Dante's achievements that he succeeded in reconciling the two great currents of European literature before they had even attained to self-consciousness. Unfortunately he found no successors capable of carrying on his achievement, with the partial exception of Petrarch and Chaucer. Otherwise we might have been saved alike from the narrow rationalism of eighteenth-century Classicism and from the emotional debauches of nineteenth-century Romanticism.

Nevertheless the age of Dante did not see the end of the Provençal influence in Italy. The troubadours and Arnaut Daniel, in particular, found a new disciple in Petrarch, and through Petrarch, who was canonized by Bembo (himself a student of Provençal) as a pillar of classical orthodoxy, the Provençal tradition entered the full stream of the Renaissance. It would need another essay to show how much the literature and culture of the Renaissance owed to this element. It is enough to say that the influence of Provencal romanticism survived the age of Aristotelian dictatorship and reappears in that last and most artificial manifestation of the courtly culture—the Italian Arcadia.[21] And before that movement had come to an end the writings of La Curne de Sainte Palaye, Dom Vaissète and Millot were preparing the way for the awakening of interest in Provençal literature and culture which played so important a part in the romantic revival from the time of Herder onwards.

[21] The subsequent revival of interest in Provençal literature actually owed much to the writings of the first president of the Arcadia, Crescimbeni. It is to him that Bodmer, for example, owes his knowledge of the troubadours.

THE VISION OF PIERS PLOWMAN

IT would be strange to write of mediaeval religion without some mention of one who is not only one of the greatest of English religious poets, but also the most remarkable and the most authentic representative of the religious sentiment of the common people of mediaeval England.

And yet for some reason William Langland has never received the attention that he deserves. He is little read, and those who read him seldom realize his true greatness. It is a reproach to modern England that when every minor poet has been edited and re-edited to satiety, and when the classics of foreign literature are to be found on every bookstall, this great classic, which is one of the landmarks of English literature and English religion, should be inaccessible to the ordinary man except in abridged or incomplete forms[1] and that the only standard work on the subject should have been written by a foreigner.[2] And this reproach ought to be felt by Catholics before all others, since for them

[1] The standard edition edited by Prof. Skeat (Oxford, 1886, 2 vols. and E.E.T.S. 4 vols.) is too expensive to be in general use. Wright's edition is both out of date and out of print. Skeat's popular edition of the text (Oxford) and his modern version (Dent), both somewhat expurgated, only contain the Prologue and the first seven *passus* (out of twenty) of the B text. Perhaps the most handy and accessible version is that by Arthur Burrell in Everyman's Library, but this is both translated and abridged. An excellent school text of the Prologue and Passus V to VII of the B text, edited by C. D. Pamely, was published by Messrs Sidgwick and Jackson in 1928. In this essay I have thought it best to give my own versions of the passages that I quote, though I do not pretend to have found a satisfactory *via media* between a literal translation and a modern paraphrase.

[2] *L' épopée mystique de William Langland*, par J. J. Jusserand, 1893.

Langland's poem is a part of their special heritage. Here is the Catholic Englishman *par excellence*, at once the most English of Catholic poets and the most Catholic of English poets: a man in whom Catholic faith and national feeling are fused in a single flame. He saw Christ walking in English fields in the dress of an English labourer, and to understand his work is to know English religion in its most autochthonous and yet most Catholic form.

It is true that there is much in Langland that is likely to prove shocking to Catholics who know their Middle Ages only in a modern bowdlerized form. His England is not the idealized Catholic England of the apologist, nor the Merry England of mediaevalist myth. It is a grim enough land where oppression and misgovernment are rife, and famine and pestilence are never far away. For Langland, with all his Christian idealism, is also a realist who does not shrink from describing in pitiless detail the corruptions of the Church, the wrongs of the poor and the vices of the rich. He belongs to his age—the fourteenth century—which, in spite of Boccaccio and Chaucer, was not a cheerful one, but which, none the less, was a time of immense spiritual vitality and of momentous consequences for the future of Western civilisation.

The fourteenth century was an age of profound social and spiritual change: an age of ruin and rebirth, of apocalyptic fears and mystical hopes. It was the age of the Great Schism and the Black Death and the Hundred Year's War, but it was also the age of Dante and Petrarch, of St Catherine and St Bridget, of Tauler and Suso and Ruysbroeck, an age of poets and mystics and saints. It saw the breakdown of the universal theocratic order of mediaeval Christendom and the rise of political nationalism and religious division, and at the same time it witnessed the passing of the old agrarian feudal society and the rise of capitalism and urban industrialism. Western Europe was stirred from end to end by a wave of social unrest which showed itself in revolutionary movements and bitter class warfare. At no other time in European history has the common people asserted itself more vigorously or found more remarkable leaders. It was the age of the Jacquerie and the Peasants' Revolt, of the wars of the Swiss peasants and the German towns against the princes, and the still more heroic struggle of the Flemish proletariat against their own ruling classes and the power of the French monarchy.

It was in the midst of this turmoil of change that the English people first attained maturity and self-consciousness. Three centuries earlier it had been submerged by a wave of foreign invasion, and the Norman conquest had made England for a time a province of continental culture. Its churchmen belonged to the international unity of Latin Christendom and its nobles to the hardly less international society of French chivalry. Latin was the language of learning, and French the language of society. English became the speech of peasants, the mark of the simple and the uneducated. As the first English chronicler, Robert of Gloucester, writes as late as the beginning of the fourteenth century: "If a man does not know French he is little esteemed, but low-born people hold still to English and their own tongue." The fourteenth century changed all that, and

before its close English was not only the language of
the people but was making its way into Court and Parliament, until in the last year of the century the first
English-speaking king opened his first Parliament in
English words. Trevisa dates the change, at least in
education, from the time of the Black Death, and no
doubt the great pestilence and the great war with France
mark a dividing line in the history of English culture.
But the vital factor in the new development was not so
much the decay of the artificial Norman-French culture as the spiritual rebirth of the national consciousness. The English genius found simultaneous expression
in the work of Chaucer and Langland, the poet of the
Canterbury Tales and the poet of *Piers Plowman*.

These two great voices of England expressed the two
aspects of English character and English culture. Chaucer represents all that England had learnt from its three
centuries of incorporation in continental culture. He
is a courtier and a scholar who looks at the English
scene with the humorous detachment of a man of the
great world. He clothed the courtly tradition in an
English dress and gave the common Englishman a right
of entry into the cultivated society which had hitherto
been the monopoly of clerks and knights.

This achievement is reflected in his style, which is so
characteristically English and his own, and yet owes so
much to the cultivation and imitation of French and
Italian models. It is essentially classical in spirit, far
more classical indeed than that of his French masters,
such as Guillaume Machaut, since it is the result of a
long process of experiment and elaborate artifice, which
bears fruit not in the wooden rhetoric of Lydgate and

Occleve or the empty grace of fifteenth-century French verse, but in a simplicity and strength that make it not incomparable with that of the great Italian classics of the Trecento.

Nothing could be more different from this than the other great work of the new age, for it is as formless and as lacking in conscious literary artifice as any great work can be. It is a voice from another world—the submerged world of the common English—a voice that is by turns harsh and pitiful and comic, but always the authentic voice of the English people. Where Chaucer took the world as he found it, and found it good, the author of *Piers Plowman* judged the world and found in wanting. He represents the English view of life as it had been formed by nearly a thousand years of Christian faith, not the official view of the theologian and the scholar, but the spiritual vision of a prophet chosen among his fellows by his inspiration alone.

And this contrast is not simply a matter of temperament or class: it has its basis in a profound difference of cultural tradition. Chaucer belongs, as I have said, to the international tradition of the courtly culture, and already has his eyes open to the dawn of the Italian Renaissance; but Langland owes nothing to the courtly tradition with its gay rhymed measures and its cult of love and romance. He looks back to the forgotten Nordic world and to the grave Christian poetry of Saxon England. He uses the old alliterative accentual measure which was the native speech of English and Teutonic poetry and which now suddenly arose, as it were from the dead, as a sign of the renaissance of the English spirit. This return to the old alliterative metre was not peculiar to Langland—we find it also in the work of Huchown of the Awle Ryale and of the poet of the *Pearl* and *Gawain*. But Langland inherited the spirit as well as the form of the old northern poetry. He has the same attitude to life —that profound and gloomy meditation on the world and the fate of man that distinguishes the old Teutonic poetry from the light-hearted courtly literature that had its origin in Provence.

There is a striking example of this in Langland's vision of "The Mountain called Middelerde";

> "And I bowed my body . beholding all about,
> And saw the sun and the sea . and the sand after,
> Where that birds and beasts . wander with their mates,
> Wild worms in the woods . and wonderful fowls
> With flecked feathers . of full many a colour.
> Man and his mate . both might I see,
> Poverty and plenty . peace and war,
> Bliss and bitter bale . both saw I at once;
> And how that men took meed . and mercy refused.
>
> .   .   .   .   .   .
>
> In sooth I saw Reason . ruling all beasts
> Save man and his mate . and thereof I wondered."[3]

Poetry such as this stands entirely outside contemporary literary tradition. Nevertheless it has its tradition, which is that of the old Teutonic literature. It has far more in common with the melancholy of Anglo-Saxon elegiac poetry or with the oracular solemnity of *Muspili* than with the smooth technical dexterity of Machaut or Froissart. And it is characteristic of the Nordic strain in Langland's poetry that his Christian

[3] C, xiv, 134-143 and 153.

epic should end, like the *Volospa* and the epics of the heathen North, on a note of defeat and despair—with the vision of a final battle for a lost cause against the unloosed hosts of hell.

On the other hand, Langland's style has none of the stately and artificial rhetoric of ancient Teutonic poetry. His language is the everyday speech of his time—at least of the friars and the popular preachers. It is full of racy vernacular turns of expression, as well as of latinisms and gallicisms borrowed from the mixed language of lawyers and clerks. Moreover, he belongs to his own age—the century of Boccaccio and Chaucer—by his interest in the spectacle of human life and his keen eye for realistic detail. And this union of profound melancholy and vivid realism shows itself in all that he wrote and imparts an extremely personal character to his poetry. There are, I know, learned men who deny the traditional authorship and the unity of the poem, and would make it the work of a whole platoon of poets. But it would be little short of a miracle if a single age had produced a succession of poets, or even two of them, with the same general attitude to the social and spiritual problems of their age and the same highly individual blend of realism and mysticism. It is true that there are considerable differences between the successive versions of the poem that have been classified by Professor Skeat as the A, B and C texts. But these are no greater than might be expected if the different versions reflect the changes of thirty years' experience; in fact, they seem to show a continuous development of thought and purpose which is entirely consistent with the author's character as he draws it himself.

Consequently I see no reason to doubt either the unity of authorship or the traditional ascription to William Langland. Langland was born about the year 1333 in the heart of that West Country that has been so rich in poets, either at Cleobury Mortimer, or, as has been recently suggested by Mr A. H. Bright, at Longlands, near Ledbury, just beneath the Malvern Hills, the scene of the opening vision of his poem.[4] According to the tradition recorded in a fifteenth-century MS. of the poem, he was the son of one Stacy de Rokayle, of Shipton-under-Wychwood, a tenant of the Despensers who held the lordship of Malvern Chase at this period. But if so, it is probable that he was a bastard, for the circumstances of his life as recorded in the auto-biographical passages that occur in the later versions of his poem are irreconcilable with his being the lawful son of a noble and wealthy house. It is very hard to reject the evidence of these passages, for they bear an unmistakable note of sincerity; and though mediaeval authors often put their views into the mouth of a fictitious or pseudonymous character, so far as I know, they never created a purely imaginary character of this type. Internal evidence shows that the second version of the poem—the B text—was written about the year 1377-8, when the author was forty-five years of age. The first version—the A text—has been assigned to the year 1362 on the strength of a reference to the great storm that occurred on January 15th of that year,[5] while the

4 *New Light on Piers Plowman*, by A. H. Bright, Oxford, 1928.
5 On the other hand, it is difficult not to see in the description of Lady Meed and her trial before the king an allusion to Alice Perrers, the mistress of Edward III, and to the events of 1376, when she was banished from Court at the instance of the Good

final version of the poem belongs to the last decade of the fourteenth century. It seems that Langland did not survive the year 1399, for a conclusion that has been added to one MS. of the A text by a certain John But before the close of the reign of Richard II, writes of him as already deceased. Consequently he cannot be the author of the poem on the fall of Richard II—*Richard the Redeless*—which was ascribed to him by Skeat, but which is a purely political poem that bears little or no trace of Langland's characteristic mentality.

The greater part of his life seems to have been spent in London, for the autobiographical passages of the poem describe the author as living "in a cot on Cornhill" with his wife and his daughter, a member of that proletariat of clerks in minor orders who earned a bare livelihood by singing office in the chantries and saying prayers for the souls of their well-to-do patrons.

"I live in London, and on London too
The looms that I labour with . my livelihood to earn
Are my paternoster and primer . *placebo* and *dirige*
And my psalter sometimes . and my seven psalms.
Thus I sing for the souls . of such as do me help,
And those that find me my food . vouchsafe, I trow,
To welcome me when I come . otherwhiles in a
    month,
Now with him and now with her . and in this way I
    beg
Without bag or bottle. but my belly only."[6]

Parliament. If this were so, however, it would make the first version almost contemporary with the second, which is difficult to believe.

[6] C, vi, 44-52.

He pictures himself as a long, lean, eccentric figure wandering through the streets of London, paying little heed to those about him, "loath to reverence lords or ladies" or to bow before men in fur coats and silver chains, and regarded by his neighbours as no better than a fool.[7] His married life seems to have been unhappy, and he was always pursued by poverty and ill-health. Thus he lived in bitterness of spirit, in failure and suffering, always feeling the contempt of men and the emptiness of his wasted life. And yet he was continually spurred on by his power of spiritual vision and by a sense that somewhere, just out of his reach, was the prize that would make up for everything, the Pearl for which a man will sell all he has. He saw himself as the unlucky speculator who has always lost but who, some day, somehow, will light on the bargain that will make him rich for ever.

> "That is sooth I said . and so I beknow
> That I have tynt [lost] time . and time mispended;
> And yet I hope as he . that oft hath chaffered,
> That aye hath lost and lost . and at last him happed
> He bought such a bargain . he was ever the better,
> And set his loss at a leaf . at the last end.
>
> .   .   .   .   .   .
>
> So hope I to have . of Him that is almighty
> A gobbet of his grace . and begin a time
> That all times of my time . to profit shall turn."[8]

Thus his poem is not a work of art like the poems of

[7] B, xv, 1-11.
[8] C, Passus vi, 92-101. The autobiographical passage of which this is the conclusion is of itself, to my mind, a sufficient refuta-

Chaucer, it is the vessel into which the poet poured his doubts, his hopes, his criticism of life and his prophetic message. There is no other work of mediaeval literature, not even the *Testaments* of Villon, which has such a direct contact with life and which gives us such an insight into the heart of mediaeval humanity. It is true that though his style owes nothing to the mediaeval romance tradition, he borrowed from that tradition the external machinery of vision and allegory. All these cumbrous personifications of virtues and vices are the lay figures that had been the stock-in-trade of mediaeval didactic literature for centuries. And yet nowhere is the irrepressible originality and realism of the English poet more apparent. These abstractions are apt suddenly to become more personal and nearer to life than even the human characters of a great poet like Chaucer. As Blake showed, the classicism of the latter makes the Canterbury Pilgrims themselves universal human types, while Langland's realism transforms his allegorical abstractions into individual men and women. Gluttony goes into the alehouse and sits on the bench with

> "Watt the warner . and his wife both,
> Tim the tinker . and twain of his prentices,
> Hick the hackneyman . and Hugh the needeler,
> Clarice of Cockslane . and the clerk of the church,
> Dawe the diker . and a dozen other;

tion of Professor Manly's view that the author of the C text was an unimaginative pedant, and that the picture of the poet himself is merely a rhetorical device.

> A ribibor, a ratoner . a raker of Chepe,[9]
> A roper, a retainer . and Rose the disher,
> Godfrey of Garlickhythe . and Gryffin the Welsh,
>   And a heap of upholsterers."[10]

And he drinks with the best of them as though he were an honest drunkard instead of a moral abstraction.

In the same way Sloth appears as a lazy priest who knows the rhymes of Robin Hood better than his *Paternoster*, and who

> "can find in a field . or in a furrow a hare
> Better than in *Beatus vir* . or *Beati omnes*
> Construe one clause well . and ken it to my parish-
> ioners,"

while Avarice is a merchant who recounts his rogueries with naive relish and apologizes for himself as a plain man who knows no French but that of the far end of Norfolk.

All this is characteristic of Langland's strength and weakness. He has no control over his pen. He is hardly launched on his sermon before reality bursts in tumultuously and turns his moral allegory into a vivid portrayal of the vulgar humanity of a fourteenth-century English crowd.

Yet this realism is not always present. He is often content to leave his allegory on a plane of frigid abstraction, and there are occasions in which Langland surpasses the Puritans themselves in the grotesqueness of his nomenclature. He tells us of a croft called "Covet-

[9] A musician (rebab-player), a rat-catcher and a Cheapside scavenger.   [10] B, v, 316-325.

not - men's - cattle - nor - wives - nor - none - of - their-
servants - that - might - annoy - them," and the children of Piers Plowman have names that are longer and
odder than those of the Barebones family. Nevertheless at any moment the flame of pure poetry may blaze
out and silence the creaking machinery of didactic
allegorism, and the artificial vision of mediaeval tradition may pass into the spiritual vision of the seer. His
art is more like that of the Hebrew prophets than that
of the modern poet, since it is not literature but the
utterance of the word that God has put into his mouth.
It is the common speech, which human folly has spoil-
ed, brought back to its true function. For speech, he
says

> "is a shoot of grace,
> And God's gleeman . and a game of heaven.
> Would never the faithful Father . (that) his fiddle
> were untempered,
> Nor his gleeman a gadabout . a goer to taverns."[11]

The one poet with whom one may compare him is
his greater predecessor, Dante, though they represent
in many respects the opposite poles of fourteenth-century literature. For Dante, no less than Langland, conceived his task in a prophetic spirit and used the convention of the vision to convey his criticism of life and
his religious ideal. Both of them felt that the world had
gone astray, and themselves with it: both had an intense faith in the Catholic way and yet were profoundly dissatisfied with the state of the Church and convinced of the need for a drastic reform. Both looked

[11] B, ix, 100-103.

for a deliverer who should set priests and people on the
right way. But Dante brought to his task all the wisdom of the schools and the art of a highly conscious
literary culture. His way was the highway of classical
tradition—the royal road of imperial Rome—and he
found his guide in Virgil and his saviour in the Messianic
Emperor, the *Messo di Dio*, who will slay the harlot and
the giant with whom she sins.

Langland, on the other hand, had the scanty learning of a poor clerk, a knowledge of the liturgy and the
Bible and the common faith of Christendom.[12] His way
was the muddy highroad of common life, and he found
his guide and saviour in the common man, Piers Plowman, who is the type of Labour and Christian charity
and at last of Christ Himself.

In *Piers Plowman* the social crisis of the age attains
clear and direct expression. It is not only the first
authentic voice of the English people, it is the first and
almost the only utterance in literature of the cry of the
poor:

"Old men and hoar . that be helpless and needy,
    And women with child . that cannot work,
    Blind men and bed ridden . and broken in their mem-
        bers,
    And all poor sufferers . patient under God's sending,
    As lepers and mendicants . men fallen into mischief,
    Prisoners and pilgrims . and men robbed perchance,
    Or brought low by liars . and their goods lost,
    Or through fire or through flood . fallen to poverty,

[12] The limitation of his learning is shown by the fact that on
one occasion he translates *ne moechaberis* as "thou shalt not kill"!

That take their mischiefs meekly . and mildly at
heart."[13]

With all its talk of class consciousness modern Social-
ism has failed to produce any work of "proletarian"
literature that is comparable to this in depth and poign-
ancy. The bitter cry of the socially disinherited against
the injustice of their lot breaks out again and again in
Langland's poem piercing through the cumbrous
superstructure of theological exhortation and moral
allegory:

"There the poor dare plead
  To have allowance of his lord . by the law he it
    claimeth,
  Joy that never Joy had . of rightful Judge he asketh
  And saith 'Lo, birds and beasts . that no bliss know-
    eth,
  And wild worms in the wood . through winter
    Thou grievest them
  And makest them well-nigh meek . and mild for
    default,
  But after Thou sendest them summer . that is their
    sovreign joy
  And bliss to all that be . both wild and tame.
  Then may beggars like beasts . ask after bliss
  That all their life have lived . in languor and in
    dearth.'
  But God send them some time . some manner joy,
  Either here or elsewhere . else were it ruth,
  For amiss he were made . who was made not for
    joy."[14]

[13] C, x, 175-183. [14] C, xvi, 289-301 (B, xiv, 108-120).

Or again in a passage which I do not wish to weaken by translation:

> "Ac pore peple, thi prisoneres . in the put of myschief,
> Conforte tho creatures . that moche care suffren
> Thorw derth, thorw drouth . alle her dayes here,
> Wo in wynter tymes . for wantyng of clothes,
> And in somer tyme selde . soupen to the fulle;
> Comforte thi careful . Chryst, in thi ryche,
> For how Thow confortest alle creatures . clerkes
>   bereth witnesse."[15]

But Langland is not merely alive to the sufferings of the poor, he is also intensely conscious of the social changes that accompanied the introduction of the new economic order and the evils that they brought in their wake. He was loyal to the old hierarchical ideal of a society based on custom and loyal service, and looked askance at the new power of money that was transforming the world. In his vision of Lady Meed, which occupies the first part of his poem, he draws a picture of a society intoxicated by the power of wealth and governed by purely economic motives. The Lady Meed is nothing more or less than the power of the purse.

> "Trust in her treasure . betrayeth full many,
> She hath poisoned Popes . and impaired Holy
>   Church.
> Monks and minstrels . are among her lovers,
> Both learned men . and lepers in hedges.
> Summoners and jurymen . are such as prize her,

[15] B, xiv, 174-9.

She is with the sheriffs . who rule the shires;
For she robs men of their lands . and their life as well,
And giveth the gaoler . gold and silver
To unfetter the false . to fly where he will.
And taketh true men by the top . and tieth them fast,
And hangeth them for hatred . that never did harm.
To be cursed in consistory . she counteth not a straw;
For she gives a cope to the commissioner . and coats
    to his clerks;
She is assoiled of sin . as soon as she will.
In a single month . she can do as much
As the privy seal . can do in six score days,
For she is privy with the Pope . provisors know it,
Simony and she . seal their bulls.
She blesseth these bishops . though they be unlearn-
    ed,
Promoteth parsons . and giveth protection to priests,
To keep lemans and lotebies . all their life days,
And to bring forth bairns . against the law's biddings.
Where she is well with the king . woe is the realm."[16]

In reply to this arraignment Lady Meed defends herself by an appeal to the universality and sovereignty of the economic motive:

"It becometh a king . that keepeth a realm,
To give Meed to men . who serve him meekly,
To aliens, and to all men . to honour them with gifts,
Meed maketh him beloved, . and esteemed as a man.
Emperors and earls . all manner of lords,
By Meed get yeomen . to run and ride.
The Pope and all prelates . take gifts and presents,

[16] B, iii, 123, 127, 132-152.

And give Meed to men . to maintain their laws.
Servants for their service . take Meed of their masters:
Beggars for their prayers . beg for Meed in return;
Minstrels for their mirth . Meed they ask.
The king hath Meed of his men . to make peace in
    the land;
Men that teach children . crave of them Meed.
Priests that preach good words to the people
Ask Meed and mass pence . and their meat at meal
    times.
All kinds of craftsmen . crave Meed for their pren-
    tices;
Merchants and Meed . must needs go together,
No wight as I ween . without Meed may live."[17]

Against all this Langland sets his vision of a new age,
when Truth shall return and "Love shall be leader in
the land."

"No more shall Meed . be the mistress as now,
But love and lowliness . and loyalty together,
These shall be lords in the land . truth to save.

    .   .   .   .   .   .

And kind-love shall come yet . and conscience to-
    gether,
And make law a labourer . such love shall arise,
And such a peace among the people . and so perfect a
    truth,
That Jews shall ween in their wits . and wax won-
    drous glad,
That Moses or Messias . be come into this earth,

[17] B, iii, 208-226.

And have wonder in their hearts . that men be so
    true."[18]

This apocalyptic hope of a spiritual renewal of
Christendom was characteristic of the central period of
the Middle Ages. It attained peculiarly clear expression
with Joachim of Flora and with the Spiritual Franciscans,
but it is also found in almost every quarter of the
mediaeval world—among mystics like Mechtild of
Magdeburg and Rulman Merswin and also among
men of letters like Dante and Petrarch and even among
politicians such as Cola di Rienzo, as well as among
countless obscure visionaries and reformers of whom
Langland is the spokesman. But Langland expresses
this current of ideas in a new spirit of ethical realism that
is characteristically English. His interests are more
social than those of the mystics, while they are less
political than those of Dante or Rienzo. He saw the
need of his time primarily as a social need for a spiritual
remedy. Society was diseased, and the only cure for its
sickness was to be found in Christianity. The tragedy
of the age was that although Christianity was nominally supreme and was surrounded by all the pomp and
external recognition that society could give it, it seemed powerless to change human life. Christ had been
proclaimed king, but He was king in name only; the
real sovereign was Lady Meed, who was honoured by
clergy and nobles, while Christ stood without in the
dress of the poor.

    "And now is ruth to rede . how the red noble
                [18] B, iii, 288-290, 297-302.

Is reverenced before the rood . and received for the
   worthier
Than Christ's cross, that o'ercame . death and deadly
   sin.
Both rich and religious . reverence that rood
That is graven on groats . and on gold nobles.[19] . . .

It seemeth now soothly . to the world's sight
That God's word worketh not . on learned or on
   lewd
But in such manner as Mark . meaneth in the gospel:
'If the blind lead the blind . both shall fall into the
   ditch'."[20]

That is why Langland's anger is so hot against the
new Scribes and Pharisees, the men who sit in Moses'
seat and bind burdens on the people which they will
not touch themselves. He describes the fat theologian
who has just preached before the Dean of St Paul's on
the sufferings of the apostle "*in fame et frigore* and flappe
of scourges," sitting down himself at the high table and
gorging on wild boar and tripe and pies and puddings,
while the poor man sups below on a sour loaf.[21] He
describes the rich men arguing on religious matters
"at meat in their mirth when minstrels are still."

"Thus they drivel on their dais . the Deity to know
   And gnaw God in their gullet . when their guts are
      full.
   But the careful may cry . and complain at the gate
   Both a-hungered and athirst . quaking with cold
   Is none to call him near . to help his need.

[19] B, xv, 501-3, 506-8.   [20] B, x, 274-6.   [21] B, xiii, 60-110.

But they hue him away like a hound . and order him
   off.

.   .   .   .   .   .

God is much in the mouths . of these great masters,
But among mean men . His mercy and works."[22]

In Langland's eyes the only true religion is a religion
of works, and the only works that avail are works of
charity.

"For though you be true of your tongue . and earn
   truly,
And as chaste as a child . that weepeth in church,
But save you love loyally . and lend to the poor,
And such goods as God sends you . give in goodly
   fashion.
You have no more merit . in Mass nor in Hours
Than hath Malkyn of her maidenhood . that no man
   desireth.
For James the gentle . judged in his book
That Faith without Fact[23] . is right nothing worth
And as dead as a doornail . except deeds follow.
Therefore Chastity without charity . will be chained
   in Hell,
It is as lacking as a lamp . with no light in it."[24]

Langland's aim is to bring religion out of the palace
and the pulpit into direct contact with common humanity. He wants to strip it of its rich vestments, its pious
knick-knacks and its load of useless learning, and set it
to work in the slums and the highways, clearing up the
mess that had been accumulated by generations of

[22] B, x, 51-70.   [23] i.e., works, deeds.   [24] B, i, 177-187.

neglect. This ideal is embodied in the symbolic figure that has given its name to the whole poem. While Dante, a type of the political idealist, puts his faith in the coming of a prince

> "Who may far off behold
> Of the True City the eternal towers,"

Langland finds the man who will put the world right in the shape of an English farmer, ploughing his half-acre by the wayside. Piers Plowman is at first simply the type of honest husbandry, a mediaeval John Bull who does his duty by Church and State and has no use for beggars or lazy workmen. But he is John Bull spirit-ualised, "Truth's pilgrim at the plough for poor men's sake," whose mission it is to bring Christendom back into the way of salvation.

Thus the conception of Piers Plowman is a composite one which includes both a sociological and a theological element. Piers is primarily the peasant who works for all and toils to win the harvest that the idle waste. He is the true economic foundation of society, as opposed to Meed, which is the false economic motive. But also since the poor stand nearest to God,

> "And in the apparel of a poor man . and a pilgrim's likeness
> Many times God has been met . among needy peo-ple,"

Piers Plowman stands for none other than Christ Him-self, the pattern of divine charity.

> "Therefore not by looks nor by learning . shalt thou know charity,

Neither by words nor by works . but by one will
   only,
And that knoweth no clerk . nor creature on earth,
But Piers the Plowman . *Petrus, id est, Christus.*
For he is not in lollers[25] . or land leaping hermits
Nor at anchorholds with an alms box . all such are
   deceivers.
For charity is God's champion . and gentle as a good
   child,
And the merriest of mouth . where he sitteth at meat.
The love that lieth in his heart . maketh him light of
  . speech,
And he is companionable and comfortable . as Christ
   Himself.
I have seen him in silk . and sometime in russet,
Both in gray and in fur . and in gilt armour,
And gladly he gave . to all men that needed.
Edmund and Edward . each was a king,
And set as saints . for following of charity.
I have seen charity also . singing and preaching,
Running and riding . in ragged weeds,
But bidding as a beggar . behold I him never,
But in rich robes . rather he walks,
Both capped and chrisomed . with shaven crown
And cleanly clothed . in cipress and silk.
And in a friar's frock . once was he found,
But it is far ago . in St Francis' time."[26]

Here the conception definitely transcends all class
limitations and becomes as wide and universal as char-

[25] Literally *idlers*, but also used as equivalent to the Latin *Lol-lardus*.   [26] B, xv, 203-226.

ity itself. Nevertheless Langland does not entirely
abandon the sociological aspect of his figure. The last
section of the poem, the vision of Dobest, opens with
the passage in which he dreams

"That Piers the Plowman . was painted all bloody,
And came in with a cross . before the common
    people,
Like in all limbs . to our Lord Jesus,"

and goes on to treat of Piers as the symbol of St Peter
and the Church. But presently there is an approxima-
tion to the Piers Plowman of the earlier visions in the
speech of the "ignorant curate" who wishes that conscience should be the keeper of the king's court and
grace the guide of the clergy:

"And Piers with his new plough . and eke with his old,
Emperor of all the world . so that all men should be
    Christian,
Imperfect is the Pope . that should help all people,
Yet sendeth men to slay . such as he should save.[27]

.   .   .   .   .   .

But blessed be Piers Plowman . who toileth to till
As well for the wastrel . and the wench of the stews,
As for himself and his servants . save that he is first
    served.

[27] This probably refers to "The War of the Eight Saints" between Gregory XI and the Florentines in 1376-8, especially to
the massacre perpetrated at Cesena in 1377 by Cardinal Robert
of Geneva, the future Pope Clement VII, in which the English
mercenaries were concerned and which aroused much indignation at the time.

And travailleth and tilleth . for a traitor as sore
As for a true tidy man . all times alike."[28]

Thus the figure of Piers Plowman has both theological and economic implications and stands for an ideal
of social and spiritual renewal—a drastic reformation
of both Church and State. It is obvious that such an
ideal is not devoid of revolutionary potentialities, and
it seems at first sight easy enough to connect it with the
two revolutionary movements that were making
themselves felt in England in Church and State at the
very time when the poem was being written; I mean
the Revolt of the Peasants and the Wyclifite movement.

Now there can be no question but that Langland's
allegory made a strong appeal to the minds of the dis-
contented peasants. Not only was the poem in itself
an expression of the new social consciousness that also
inspired the revolt, but we have direct evidence of its
use for propagandist purposes by the leaders of the
movement. The famous manifesto of John Ball to the
commons of Essex calls on Piers Plowman to go to his
work and chastise Hob the Robber, and it concludes
with yet another reference to the poem:

"And *DoWell* and *Better* and flee sin
And seek peace and hold therein.
And so bid John Trueman and all his fellows."[29]

Nevertheless there is no reason to suppose that Langland was himself a revolutionary or in sympathy with

[28] C, xxii, 428-31, 436-441.
[29] Thomas Walsingham, *Hist. Angl.*, ii, 33 (Rolls series).

the aims of the insurgents. In the first version of the poem, written long before the rising, there is a curious passage dealing with the exorbitant demands of the working classes:

"Labourers that have no land . to live on but their
    hands,
Deign not to dine any day . on yesterday's cabbage.
No penny-ale pleases him . nor no piece of bacon,
But he must feed on fresh meat . or fish that is fried,
Both *chaud* and *plus-chaud* . for the chill of his maw.
Save he have high wages . else will he chide,
Woe on the time . that he was born a workman,
And curse against the king . and all his council,
For allowing such laws . labourers to grieve."[30]

While in the later versions of the poem he writes against the propagation of communist ideas by the Friars, who

"Preach men of Plato . and prove it by Seneca
That all things under heaven . ought to be in com-
    mon.
And yet he lieth, as I believe . that to the lewd so
    preacheth,
For God made men a law . and Moses it taught:
Thou shalt not covet thy neighbour's goods."[31]

Langland is in fact thoroughly English in the way in which he combines an intense class-consciousness and a hatred of social injustice with a strong conservatism and a respect for the established order. He has the traditional conservative prejudice against the middle classes

[30] A, vii, 295-303.   [31] B, xx, 273-6.

—against the lawyers and officials, above all, "who would do more for a dozen chickens or a sack of oats than for the love of Our Lord or all his dear saints,"[32] but also against the merchants, who get little pardon, and against the shopkeepers,

"The men who do most harm in the world
To the poor people . who purchase piecemeal,
For they grow rich by retail . and buy rents
With that which the poor . should put in their belly."[33]

On the other hand, he is no leveller. He holds king-ship and knighthood in high honour, and accepts the traditional Christian ideal of society as a hierarchical order that has its pattern in heaven.

"When God began heaven . in that great bliss
He made knights in His court . creatures ten
Cherubim and seraphim . seven such and another."[34]
"Kings and knights . should keep the truth,
Riding and roaming . the realm around,
And take transgressors . and tie them fast,
Till truth has determined . their trespass to the end.
That is the proper profession . that pertaineth to
    knights,
And not to fast on Fridays . for fivescore winters,
But to help him and her . that hold by the truth
And never leave them for love . or for lacking of
    silver."[35]

Such an ideal had indeed little in common with the practice of the fourteenth century, and Langland

[32] A, iii, 71-5.   [33] C, ii, 104-6.   [34] B, iv, 37-9.
[35] B, i, 94-101 (C, ii, 90-101).

laments the degeneracy of his own post-war period, when gentle blood is of little account in comparison with money, when "Soapmakers and their sons are made knights for silver" and lord it over the sons of the old families that have mortgaged their estates in the national cause during the Great War in France.[36]

But though Langland is no democrat in the modern sense he remains a great exponent of the ideals of Christian democracy in the sense in which it has been defined by Leo XIII.[37] Indeed, nowhere else in English literature, nor even perhaps anywhere in the literature of Catholic Europe, do we find these ideals so clearly and passionately expressed. For Langland's social consciousness is rooted in his religious faith and finds its ultimate ground in the doctrine of Christian brotherhood:

"For all we are Christ's creatures . and of his coffers rich,
And brethren as of one blood . as well beggars as earls,
For on Calvary of Christ's blood . Christendom gan spring,
And blood brethren we became there . of one body won,
As *quasimodo geniti* . and gentlemen each one,
No beggar or serving-boy among us . save sin made us so."[38]

Thus Langland's social teaching is not based on

[36] C, vi, 72-5 (not in A and B).
[37] In his Encyclical *Graves de Communi* (1901).
[38] B, xi, 192-7, cp. B, xix, 38-40, "Those that became Christians—Are franklins and freemen . and gentlemen with Jesus."

revolutionary class hatred nor on a sentimental pity for
the unfortunate. It transcends all purely social and
economic categories, since it is nothing else but a logical
development of the central doctrine of the Christian
faith in its social implications. Langland's hope of salvation for society rests on his faith in the redemption
of humanity in the Incarnation, and his work finds its
true culmination in the great vision of the Harrowing
of Hell which is justly regarded as the finest passage in
the whole poem:

> "For I that am Lord of Life . love is my drink,
> And for that drink to-day . I died upon earth;
> But I will drink of no ditch . nor of no deep learning,
> But of the common cup . of all Christian souls;
> Though thy drink was death . and Hell the deep
>   bowl,
> I fought so that yet I thirst . for man's soul's sake;
> *Sitio.*"[39]

Here Langland is at one with the great tradition of
mediaeval mysticism and with the spirit of the universal
Church. His social ideal is not limited to his own age
and country: it is the same as that of the New Testament and that of the social encyclicals of Leo XIII and
his successors—the realisation of the Kingdom of God
on earth and the restoration of all things in Christ.

But if his social teaching is thoroughly Catholic,
what of his attitude to the Church and the Papacy? Are
his bitter complaints against the corruption of the clergy
and his demand for drastic reforms reconcilable with
orthodoxy? Or should they be regarded as part of the

[39] C, xxi, 406-411; B, xviii, 363-6.

same movement of religious disaffection and revolt which culminated in England during Langland's lifetime in the heresy of Wyclif and the Lollards? It is easy enough to understand how later Protestant ages should have taken this view, as, for example, when Thomas Fuller hails the poet as the morning star of the Reformation, belonging rather to the day than to the night. Langland's criticism of the degeneracy of the religious orders is alone sufficient to explain this, above all the famous prophecy which enjoyed such popularity in Tudor times:

"But yet shall come a king . and confess you all,
And beat you, as the Bible telleth . for breaking of
    your rule.
And amend you monks . moniales and canons,
And put you to your penance . *ad pristinum statum ire.*

·   ·   ·   ·   ·   ·

For the abbot of England . and the abbess his niece
Shall have a knock on their crowns . and incurable
    the wound,
But ere that king come . as chronicler me told,
Clerks and Holy Church . shall be clothed anew."[40]

But it is not difficult to find parallels to this passage in mediaeval writers of the most unblemished orthodoxy, notably in the no less famous prophecy of St Hildegard two centuries before.[41]

But the resemblances between Langland and Wyclif

[40] C, vi, 169-172, 177-180 (B, x, 317-329).
[41] I am inclined to think that this prophecy is the source of Langland's lines, as it was well known in the fourteenth century and is often referred to by Wyclif.

go much further than this. Not only do we find in both
of them the same attitude of hostility to the religious
orders, above all the Friars; the same contempt for
pardoners and pilgrimages; the same attacks on the
financial corruption of the Papacy and the Curia; and
the same belief in the evil effects on the Church of
excessive wealth and the desirability of a measure of
disendowment by the secular power; but the resemblance often extends to matters of detail and turns of expression. For instance, Wyclif's complaints of the
bishops *in partibus* who, instead of going to their dio-
ceses abroad and converting the heathen, carry on an
easy and lucrative business as suffragan bishops in England, has its exact counterpart in Langland's lines about
the need for preaching the faith to the Saracens, the
neglect of which is:

"A peril to the Pope . and the prelates that he maketh,
That bear bishops' names . of Bedlam and Babylon
Who hip about in England . to hallow men altars
And creep among curates . and confess against the
    law
'Put not your sickle into another man's harvest'."[42]

Or again, Langland's description of the rich eccles-
iastic riding through the land on a fine horse with his
sword on his thigh and his hounds at his back, is repeated in Wyclif's writings in almost identical terms.[43]

[42] B, xv, 537 seq.
[43] B, x, 306-316 and Wyclif, English Works, ed. Matthew,
121, 149, 151, 212-3, 434; *de Blasphemia*, 188; Select English
Works ed. Arnold, III, 519.
Other instances are their common views on marriage and the

It is not, however, in passages like these that either the originality or the heresy of Wyclif is to be found. The demand for reformation and the denunciation of ecclesiastical corruption were not peculiar to the Lollards; they are characteristic of the whole period. It was the custom of the Middle Ages to use strong language, and they had none of the modern prejudice against washing dirty linen in public. As Dr Owst has pointed out,[44] many things that we regard as characteristic of Wyclif or characteristic of Langland were the commonplaces of the contemporary pulpit, and it is easy to find similar views no less strongly expressed in the writings of champions of orthodoxy like Bishop Brunton, and the Dominican John Bromyard, who took part in the Council at Blackfriars in 1382, which condemned Wyclif's heresies. And it is here rather than in the writings of Wyclif, which were posterior at least to the first version of *Piers Plowman*, that we should look for the source of Langland's views.

Where Langland agrees with Wyclif is precisely where the latter was in agreement with English popular opinion. As we have seen, the second half of the fourteenth century saw the first complete emergence of the English national consciousness, which expressed itself in a widespread movement for reform in Church and State. This movement finds a clear expression in

evil of marrying for money instead of for love: Wyclif, ' Of Wedded Men and Wives," *Select English Works*, III, 188-201; *Piers Plowman*, A, x, 106; B, ix, 150 seq.: and their criticism of the Pope levying war on Christians, etc.

[44] G. R. Owst, *Preaching in Mediaeval England* (1926), pp. xii, 36, 131, and on Langland, 295-6. Also *Literature and Pulpit in Mediaeval England* (1933), ch. ix.

the proceedings of Parliament in the later years of Edward III and reached its climax in the Good Parliament of 1376, where for the first time the Commons took a leading part. Now, as Jusserand has pointed out, Langland's views reflect those of the Commons to such a degree that his poem often reads like a poetical commentary on the Rolls of Parliament.[45] "In religious, as in secular matters, Langland sides not with Wyclif, but heart and soul with the Commons of England."

"Like the Commons, he recognizes the religious authority of the Pope, but protests against Papal encroachments and against the interference of the Sovereign Pontiff in temporal matters. The extension assumed by the Papal power in England appears to him excessive; like the Commons he is in favour of the statutes of Provisors and Praemunire, and wishes to have them maintained and renewed ... In questions of this kind Langland often agrees with Wyclif; but it will usually be found that both share on these points the ideas of Parliament."[46]

One petition in particular which deals with the evil effects of simony and non-residence shows a remarkable similarity to the dominant theme of Langland's vision of Lady Meed. In the past, say the Commons, benefices were conferred on worthy men who stayed in their cures and spent the goods of Holy Church in works of charity. "And as long as these good customs were observed the kingdom was filled with all kinds of prosperity, such as good people and loyal clerks and clergy, knights and chivalry, which are things that

[45] J. Jusserand, *Piers Plowman* (Eng. trans., 1894), p. 112 and 71.
[46] *Ibid.*, p. 128, cf. pp. 129-136.

always go together, peace and quiet, treasure, wheat, cattle and other riches. But since the good customs have been perverted into the sin of covetousness and simony, the kingdom has been full of divers adversities, such as wars and pestilence, famine, murrain of cattle and other ills."[47]

And Langland expresses the same idea in poetical language:

> "Neither the sea nor the sand . nor the seed yieldeth
> As they were wont . in whom is the fault?
> Not in God nor in the ground . that they are good no
>   longer;
> And the sea and the seed . the sun and the moon
> Do their duty day and night . and if we did also
> There should be plenty and peace . perpetual for ever."

But

> "Now faileth the folk of the flood . and the folk of the
>   land,
> Shepherd and shipmen . and so do the tillers,
> No more can they ken . the course of the seasons."[48]

Neither Langland nor the commons desire revolutionary changes or the subversion of hierarchical authority, but a return to the sacred order on which society rested, according to mediaeval ideas. The Middle Ages were always striving towards this ideal and were never satisfied that they had attained it. And it was above all with regard to the reform of the Church that this tendency shows itself. The real Age of the Re-

---

[47] Rot. Parl., ii, 337 in Jusserand, op. cit., 133-4.
[48] C, xviii, 90-93; B, xv, 360-2 (C, xviii, 103-4).

formation was not the sixteenth century but the whole
later mediaeval period from the eleventh century onwards. It was inevitable that such a movement should
produce extremists and enthusiasts who ultimately
passed into schism or heresy, as was the case with Arnold
of Brescia and Peter Waldo, and the Spiritual Franciscans and Ockham and Wyclif. Nevertheless the movement as a whole was essentially Catholic and found its
centre and base in the reformed Papacy.

But in the fourteenth century this was no longer the
case. The alliance between the Papacy and the reformers was temporarily broken and the disruptive
element in the reforming movement got the upper
hand. The Papacy ceased to be the centre of unity and
became itself the victim of schism.

It was not, however, the Great Schism so much as the
translation of the Papacy to Avignon that marked the
turning-point, by destroying the super-national prestige
of the Holy See. It is true that the Popes of Avignon
did not deserve the indiscriminate condemnation that
was passed upon them by contemporary writers like
Villani and Petrarch. They included men of high
character and ability, such as Benedict XII and Urban
V, who were not unmindful of their universal responsibilities. Nevertheless the divorce of the Holy See
from the sacred associations of the Holy City had a
disastrous effect on public opinion. The charismatic
aspect of the Papacy fell into the background, and
Avignon came to be regarded simply as the centre of a
vast bureaucratic and fiscal organisation which was
governed by financial rather than spiritual motives. It
was in the words of the Good Parliament, "*La peccher-*

ouse cité d' Avenon," where "brokers of benefices" and worldly cardinals lived in shameful luxury on the exploitation of the faithful.

This state of things produced a situation in which it is far more difficult to draw a sharp line of division between the movement of Catholic reform and the heretical tendency to revolt than at any other period in the Church's history. This is seen, above all, in the Spiritual Franciscan movement, which embodied so much of the spiritual ideals of the age, while its extreme forms produced the most extravagant types of mediaeval unorthodoxy. But it is also characteristic in a greater or less degree of all the representatives of the religious thought of the age. A canonized saint like St Bridget can denounce the Pope in unmeasured terms as "a murderer of souls, more unjust than Pilate and more cruel than Judas,"[49] while Dante can speak at times as if the Church had apostatized and had forfeited the divine guidance. On the other hand, some of the most characteristic doctrines of heretics, like Wyclif's theory of dominion and grace, are borrowed almost without alteration from the writings of orthodox prelates, like Richard Fitzralph, the Archbishop of Armagh.

In these circumstances it is not surprising that we should find many points of resemblance between the writings of Wyclif and those of Langland. Both were children of the same age, who had grown up under the same spiritual influences and who reacted against the same abuses. Both, in spite of their hostility to the Friars, were strongly influenced by Franciscan ideas.

[49] *Rev.* i, c. 41.

And yet no two men could be more dissimilar in character and spirit. Wyclif, the famous doctor, with his ponderous learning and his bitter tongue, has all the faults and virtues of the Puritan reformer—a narrow mind, harsh, unbending, arrogant, austere, which, in spite of its genuine religious earnestness, lacks human warmth and spiritual sympathy. Langland, the poor clerk, has none of Wyclif's self-righteousness or his strength of purpose; he always pictures himself as a poor feckless creature labouring under a sense of inferiority and spiritual maladjustment.

"Woe-weary and wetshod . went I forth after,
As a reckless wretch . that recks not of sorrow
And fared forth like a losel . all my life-time
Till I waxed weary of this world . and willed oft to
    sleep."[50]

Yet he has passion and pity and a profound sympathy for common humanity. He can see the squalor and absurdity of life without losing sight of the spiritual realities that lie behind the surface of existence. For all his bitterness of heart, he was a man of charity, and a man of faith in spite of his tendency to doubt and despair. And so, while Wyclif became the harbinger of religious revolt, Langland embodies the spiritual unity of the English people at the very moment when religion in England stood at the parting of the ways.

For the English Church never really recovered from the crisis of the fourteenth century. The next age was an age of moral and spiritual decline. We had no San Bernardino to restore the old alliance between the

[50] C, xxi, 1-4.

Papacy and the party of reform, and no St Joan to rally the nation to unity in the name of God. Instead we had tough prelate-politicians like Beaufort and Morton and Wolsey and the men who helped to burn St Joan and to pillory well-meaning reformers like Bishop Pecocke. Only in the following century did the movement of Catholic reform reappear with Colet and Fisher and More. But it was then too late to avert the crisis. The English way diverged from the Catholic way and ran astray into the waste lands of sectarianism. The spiritual successors of Langland are to be found not in the Catholic Church, nor even in the Church of England, but among the Puritans and the rebels, with Fox and Bunyan and Whitfield and Blake. But this popular tradition of English religion which was divorced from Catholic unity and even from the national unity after the sixteenth century already exists in its purest and most unadulterated form in the work of Langland. He shows us what English religion might have been, if it had not been broken by schism and narrowed by sectarianism and heresy. Langland himself was not unconscious of the impending crisis. In the last pages of his poem he foretells the coming apostasy, when the rich and the learned would follow the standard of Antichrist and only the fools would be left to stand by the unity of Holy Church. He pictures in prophetic words the new pagan pride of life that was to replace the old ideals of Christian chivalry:

> "Loud laughed Life . . .
> And armed him in haste . with words of harlotry
> And held Holiness for a jest . and Courtesy for a
> waster,

And Loyalty a churl . and Liar a gentleman,
Conscience and Counsel . he counted it a folly."[51]

And in despair Langland calls on his fellows, the
common people, to make a last stand for the cause of
Catholic unity:

". . . come with me ye fools,
Into Unity of Holy Church . and hold we us there,
And cry we to Nature . to come and defend
Us Fools from the fiend . for the love of Piers Plow-
    man,
And call we to all the commons . that they come into
    Unity,
And there abide and do battle . against Belial's chil-
    dren."[52]

[51] C, xxiii, 143-147.   [52] C, xxiii, 74-9.